P9-CEL-983

SEASON'S
GREETINGS

SEASON'S GREETINGS

COOKING AND ENTERTAINING FOR THANKSGIVING, CHRISTMAS, AND NEW YEAR'S

MARLENE SOROSKY

Photographs by Geoffrey Nilsen

CHRONICLE BOOKS
SAN FRANCISCO

Text copyright © 1986, 1997 by Marlene Sorosky.
Photographs copyright © 1997 by Geoffrey Nilsen.
All rights reserved. No part of this book may be
reproduced in any form without written permission
from the publisher.

ISBN 0-8118-1668-0

Printed in Mexico.

Designed by Aufuldish & Warinner

CHRONICLE BOOKS
85 Second Street
San Francisco, California 94105

✳ ✳ ✳
CONTENTS
✳ ✳ ✳

ACKNOWLEDGMENTS

My deepest thanks to several people whose talents and caring enhanced my book:

Edon Waycott for helping me create and test recipes. Jim Gabrielson for his expertise with the floral arrangements, wreaths, garlands, and centerpieces. Carol Willardson, Barbara Meisner, and Ann Natwick for testing recipes. Ed and Nan Bang-Knudsen for putting me in touch with Chronicle Books and making this edition of the book come to life. Cheryl Branman, Caryn Weaver, Marjorie Morrison, and Ken Sorosky for their unwavering love and support and for the years they gave up hamburgers and hot dogs to test my "gourmet" dinners.

A big thank-you to Geoffrey Nilsen for his brilliant photographs and to Robert Lambert for his creative and exceptional food styling.

And last but not least to the memory of Bob Stein, whose beautiful photographs, dedication to excellence and commitment to perfection so greatly enhanced the original version of this book.

SEASON'S GREETINGS! The words themselves bring to mind pictures of family gatherings, stores decorated with garlands and lights, traditional holiday songs, beautifully wrapped presents under a tree and, of course, the wonderful and unforgettable smells coming from the kitchen. Everyone looks forward to the holidays, beginning with the Thanksgiving feast and continuing until the New Year's celebrations are over. It is during this time that those once-a-year foods are prepared with an extra ounce of love for family and friends. It doesn't matter whether you're the one planning and cooking the special meal or one of the lucky ones who simply enjoy the scrumptious tastes and smells—there's something about the holiday season that brings childlike excitement to both adults and youngsters. In *Season's Greetings* I have put together a collection of not only the recipes that will ensure a delicious feast, but also complete menus, table decorations, party themes, gifts to make, and holiday ideas. If your holidays are rooted in well-established family customs, you'll delight in the traditional time-proven recipes. If you're just beginning to set new family traditions, you'll find many recipes and ideas to inspire you, allowing your own creative touch to lead the way. One thing is for sure: the chapters in *Season's Greetings* provide a one-stop compilation of memorable visions and flavors guaranteed to make your holidays a delicious and happy time for all. Enjoy!

GETTING
IN THE
SPIRIT

GETTING IN THE SPIRIT

Thick fruited jams,

cakes luscious and sweet,

Baskets overflowing

with holiday treats,

Fresh homemade breads,

sauces tempting and tart,

Gifts from the kitchen

bring warmth to the heart.

Marlene Sorosky

ALTHOUGH the hustle and bustle of crowded stores at Christmastime may add to the holiday spirit, it's nice to keep your exposure to it at a minimum. While everyone else is frantically searching for that perfect last-minute gift, you will take great satisfaction in knowing your pantry shelves and freezer are filled with delectable homemade gifts. This chapter includes a bounty of gourmet goodies no one else can give and everyone will be thrilled to receive. Gifts from your own kitchen contain an extra ingredient no store can match—the heartfelt personal touch. Many of the recipes included here benefit from being made ahead. Fruitcakes taste much better and moister after they've soaked up the spirits they've been wrapped in for several months. Homemade liqueurs assembled in the fall will reach their flavorful peak by Christmas. And vinegars can

safely be prepared months ahead, using the herbs or berries of the season. In order to make the jams and preserves throughout the year, I supplement year-round fruits with frozen and canned ones, but feel free to substitute fresh when available. Whatever you choose to make ahead, you'll be so glad you did, whether you offer them as holiday treats for you and your family or as gifts for others.

DRIED-FRUIT FRUITCAKE

A Christmas cousin to apple pie, this moist cake contains dried apples, apple juice, applesauce, and spices. Baked in a bundt pan, it serves a crowd. Baked in loaf pans, it makes great gifts.

2 cups (about 6 ounces) finely chopped
    dried apples
1½ cups (about 6 ounces) chopped
    dried apricots
1½ cups (about 8 ounces) halved pitted dates
1 cup currants
1 cup dark raisins
½ cup apple juice
1 cup sugar
½ pound (2 sticks) butter or margarine,
    at room temperature
6 large eggs, at room temperature
3 cups all-purpose flour
1 teaspoon baking powder
1 tablespoon ground cinnamon
1 teaspoon ground nutmeg
1 teaspoon ground allspice
1 jar (15 ounces) applesauce
1 cup (about 4 ounces) chopped walnuts
⅓ cup brandy

❋ Preheat the oven to 300 degrees. Grease a 10-inch tube pan or bundt pan, or two 8 x 4 x 2-inch loaf pans.

❋ Mix the dried apples, apricots, dates, currants, raisins, and apple juice in a medium bowl; let stand for 1 hour. Cream the sugar and butter in a mixing bowl with an electric mixer until light and creamy. Add the eggs, one at a time, beating well after each. Add the flour, baking powder, cinnamon, nutmeg, allspice and applesauce, mixing on low speed until incorporated. Stir in the fruit mixture and nuts. Pour the mixture into the prepared pan.

❋ Bake for 2 hours, or until a cake tester inserted in the middle of the cake comes out clean. Cool 30 minutes. Go around the sides with a knife and invert onto a cooling rack. Turn right side up and cool completely.

❋ Soak a large piece of cheesecloth in brandy. Wrap the cake in the cloth and then in foil. Store in a cool place. Remoisten the cloth with brandy every couple of weeks or as necessary.

MAKES 1 LARGE ROUND OR 2 SMALLER LOAF CAKES

MAKING FRUITCAKES

Be creative. Fruitcakes allow lots of room for experimentation. For dried fruits, consider apricots, prunes, pears, peaches, figs, dates, pineapple, currants, dark or light raisins or apples. For fresh, try pears, oranges, pineapple, papaya, mango, apples, or banana. Vary the flavor of the batter by adding ribbons of almond paste, butterscotch, dark or white chocolate chips, nuts, spices, citrus peel, fruit juices, and liqueurs.

PEACH FRUITCAKE

This recipe is exceptional. Three surprise ingredients—canned peaches, mincemeat, and apricot brandy—help make it so.

2½ cups all-purpose flour
1 cup packed light brown sugar
1 teaspoon baking soda
1 teaspoon ground cinnamon
½ teaspoon ground cloves
2 cups mixed candied fruits and peels
    (1 pound)
1 cup (about 4 ounces) chopped walnuts
1 cup raisins
1 can (16 ounces) peaches, drained
    and chopped
1 can (14 ounces) sweetened condensed milk
1 cup store-bought mincemeat
½ cup apricot brandy, divided

Brandy Hard-Sauce Glaze (optional)
¼ pound (1 stick) butter or margarine,
    at room temperature
1¼ cups sifted powdered sugar
2 to 3 tablespoons brandy

❋ Preheat the oven to 300 degrees. Grease and flour two 8 x 4 x 2-inch loaf pans.

❋ In a very large bowl, stir together the flour, brown sugar, baking soda, cinnamon, and cloves. Stir in the candied fruits, nuts, and raisins. Add the peaches, condensed milk, mincemeat, and ¼ cup of the brandy, stirring until well combined. Turn into the prepared pans.

❋ Bake for 2 hours, or until a cake tester inserted in the center comes out clean. Cool completely. Go around the edges of the cakes with a knife and invert onto a cooking rack.

❋ Soak a large piece of cheesecloth in the remaining ¼ cup apricot brandy. Wrap the cakes in cheesecloth and then in foil. Store in a cool place. Remoisten the cloth every 2 weeks or as necessary.

✵ Before serving, if desired, make glaze by beating the butter in a bowl with an electric mixer at medium speed until smooth and creamy. Slowly add the powdered sugar, beating until light and fluffy. Reduce the speed to low and add 2 tablespoons brandy. Mix in the remaining brandy, a teaspoon at a time, until the glaze is of pouring consistency. Drizzle over the top and sides of the cakes.

MAKES 2 CAKES

SOAKING FRUITCAKES

In the days before refrigeration, it was commonplace to wrap fruitcakes in brandy-soaked cheesecloth to preserve them. Today they are soaked for flavor and moistness, but may be wrapped in foil or put in a tin and refrigerated and frozen, if preferred. Before soaking, cool cake to room temperature. Cut a piece of cheesecloth large enough to fold in half and wrap around the entire cake. Place desired liquor in a small bowl. Soak cheesecloth in liquor and squeeze gently to remove some of the excess liquid. Wrap cake in cloth and then in foil. Store the cake in a cool, dark place. Remoisten the cloth whenever it feels dry, about every two to three weeks. If refrigerating or freezing the cakes, it is not necessary to wrap them in liquor-soaked cloth unless you want to.

CHOCOLATE FRUITCAKE

Fruitcakes can even be made to appeal to chocolate lovers. This one, which contains candied and dried fruits, comes from my friend Natalie Haughton, food editor of the *Daily News.* If you don't like candied fruits, you may omit them or substitute your favorite dried fruits.

½ cup (about 2½ ounces) chopped dates
½ cup (about 2½ ounces) chopped dried figs
½ cup dark raisins
¼ cup chopped candied cherries
¼ cup chopped candied pineapple
¼ cup plus 2 tablespoons brandy
6 tablespoons (¾ stick) butter or margarine, at room temperature
¾ cup sugar
3 large eggs, separated, at room temperature
2 ounces unsweetened chocolate, melted in top of double boiler and cooled
1 cup all-purpose flour
½ teaspoon baking powder
1½ cups (about 6 ounces) chopped pecans
¼ to ½ cup brandy, for soaking cake

✵ Place the dates, figs, raisins, cherries, and pineapple in a medium bowl. Pour ¼ cup brandy over the fruit and let the mixture stand for several hours or overnight. Do not drain. Grease one 9 x 5 x 3-inch loaf pan or three 3 x 5 x 3-inch loaf pans. Preheat the oven to 250 degrees.

✵ Cream the butter and ½ cup of the sugar in a large mixing bowl with an electric mixer until light and fluffy, about 2 minutes. Beat in the egg yolks, one at a time. Mix in the melted chocolate and remaining 2 tablespoons brandy on low speed. Add the flour and baking powder, mixing until incorporated. Mix in the fruit mixture and nuts.

✵ Beat the egg whites in a small mixing bowl with an electric mixer until foamy. Slowly beat in the remaining ¼ cup sugar, mixing until stiff but moist peaks form. Fold the whites into the batter. Pour the batter into the prepared pan(s). Bake small cakes for 1 hour and a large cake for 2¼ hours, or until a cake tester inserted in the center comes out clean.

✵ Remove from the oven and cool 20 to 30 minutes. Go around the edges with a knife and invert the cakes onto racks. Turn right side up and cool to room temperature. Wrap in a large piece of cheesecloth moistened with brandy and then wrap in foil. Store in a cool place. Remoisten the cloth with brandy every couple of weeks or as necessary.

MAKES 1 LARGE CAKE OR 3 SMALLER CAKES

LIQUORS FOR FRUITCAKES

Although brandy is the traditional choice, equal parts of other liquors may be mixed with it for flavor variation. Experiment with Amaretto, Grand Marnier, dark rum, kirsch or apricot brandy.

LABELING YOUR GIFTS

Buy pretty, decorative labels for your homemade gifts. Include with the name important information on storing and serving.

BEGIN NATURAL WREATHS IN SUMMER

To make wreaths, pick honeysuckle, wisteria and grape vines in late summer when they are green and still flexible. Gather into bunches and secure them with raffia or wire. Overlap cut ends of vines and fasten them together. Weave in any loose or straggly ends. Hang or lay flat in a dry place until brown and thoroughly dried. To make a natural wreath, attach pods, nuts, acorns, pine cones, thistles, or seeds and nut husks with stems. Accent with dried wheat, bittersweet, or dried herbs. The dried vine wreath may also be used as a base for fresh evergreens decorated with a plaid bow and Christmas balls.

LIQUEURS

ORANGE COFFEE LIQUEUR

CRANBERRY CORDIAL

APRICOT BRANDY

CHOCOLATE MINT LIQUEUR

VINEGARS

RASPBERRY VINEGAR

BLACKBERRY VINEGAR

HERB VINEGAR

ORANGE COFFEE LIQUEUR

The dynamic duo of orange and coffee is evident with just one sip of this exquisite liqueur.

2 bottles (750 milliliters each) French brandy
4 cups superfine sugar
2 oranges, rinsed and dried
80 French-roast coffee beans

❋ Pour half the brandy into a large, wide-mouthed glass jar with a lid. Stir in the sugar. Puncture the oranges with a can opener or skewer and insert a coffee bean into each hole. Put the oranges into the jar; stir well. Pour in the remaining brandy. Cover and store in a cool, dark place for 60 days, stirring occasionally.

❋ Before serving, remove and discard the oranges.

The liqueur may be kept at room temperature for up to 3 months. Refrigerate it for longer storage.

MAKES ABOUT 6 CUPS

CLEANING EMPTY BOTTLES
To rid bottles of odors, fill them half full of water. Add 1 tablespoon baking soda and shake well. Let stand for 1 hour and then rinse thoroughly.

CRANBERRY CORDIAL

Here's a festive way of using crimson cranberries during their short season. Coarsely chopped, they add vivid color and intense flavor to this liqueur. After you strain off the cordial, you will be left with brilliant brandied cranberries. Use them to make a relish or add them to your favorite fruitcake.

1 package (12 ounces) fresh cranberries
1 cup sugar
2 cups light corn syrup
2 cups vodka
1 cup water
½ cup brandy

❋ Coarsely chop the cranberries in a food processor fitted with the metal blade, or chop with a knife. Stir the cranberries and sugar in a large bowl until the berries are well coated. Stir in the corn syrup, vodka, water, and brandy until blended. Pour the mixture into a large glass jar, cover, and store in a cool, dark place for at least 1 month, stirring or shaking the jar every few days. Before serving, strain the liquid from the cranberries through a fine strainer or dampened cheesecloth.

The cordial may be tightly covered and stored at room temperature for up to 3 months. Refrigerate it for longer storage.

MAKES ABOUT 4 CUPS

APRICOT BRANDY

This liqueur, with its smooth, fruity apricot flavor, has been a longtime favorite with my holiday gift classes. As an added bonus, the apricots left from the liqueur make a superb ice cream topping or addition to a compote.

4 cups sugar
2 cups water
2 pounds dried apricots
2 bottles (750 milliliters each) vodka

❋ Bring the sugar and water to a boil in a small saucepan, stirring often. Reduce the heat and simmer 5 minutes, or until the sugar is dissolved. Cool to room temperature.

❋ Place the apricots in 1 or 2 large glass jars. Add the sugar syrup and vodka, stirring to blend. Cover tightly and store in a cool, dark place for at least 1 month, turning or shaking the jar every week. Before serving, strain the liquid.

The brandy may be stored at room temperature for up to 3 months. Refrigerate it for longer storage.

MAKES ABOUT 6 CUPS

REUSING EMPTY BOTTLES
Save empty liqueur, vinegar, chili sauce, and salad dressing bottles throughout the year and fill them with your homemade versions for gift giving. Decorate by tying plaid or colored ribbon around the neck.

CHOCOLATE MINT LIQUEUR

Two luscious after-dinner flavors make up this elegant liqueur.

Brown-Sugar Syrup
1 cup packed light brown sugar
¾ cup granulated sugar
1½ cups water

2⅔ cups vodka
2 tablespoons chocolate extract
4 teaspoons vanilla extract
1 teaspoon peppermint extract

❋ To make the brown-sugar syrup, combine sugars and water in a small saucepan. Heat to boiling, stirring often. Lower the heat and

simmer 5 minutes, or until the sugar is dissolved. Pour into a jar and cool to room temperature. The syrup may be stored in the refrigerator indefinitely.

✳ To make the liqueur, stir together the brown-sugar syrup, vodka, chocolate extract, vanilla extract, and peppermint extract in a large glass jar. Store, tightly covered, in a cool, dark place for at least 1 month.
The liqueur may be stored at room temperature for up to 3 months. Refrigerate it for longer storage.
MAKES ABOUT 5 CUPS

RASPBERRY VINEGAR

This fruity, tangy pink vinegar is just as successful in marinades and sauces as it is in salad dressings and vinaigrettes.

1 package (10 ounces) frozen raspberries
   in syrup, defrosted
48 ounces red wine vinegar

✳ Drain the raspberries, reserving 3 tablespoons syrup. Place the raspberries, vinegar, and reserved syrup in a large nonaluminum saucepan. Let stand, covered, overnight.

✳ Bring the vinegar mixture to a boil over moderately high heat. Boil, uncovered, for 3 minutes. Cool. Strain the vinegar through damp cheesecloth into a clean, hot jar. Store tightly covered for at least 2 weeks before using.
The vinegar may be stored in a cool, dark place for up to 2 months. Refrigerate it for longer storage.
MAKES 6 CUPS

BLACKBERRY VINEGAR

The dark blackberry color of this vinegar makes it exceptionally good for marinades, rather than salad dressings. Boysenberries may be substituted for the blackberries, if desired.

2 cups fresh or frozen blackberries
1 cup rice vinegar

✳ Place the berries in a wide-mouthed jar and crush them with a spoon. Pour the vinegar over, close the jar, and store in a cool, dark place for 3 days, stirring once a day. Pour the mixture through damp cheesecloth, pressing on the pulp. Discard the seeds and pulp. Pour the liquid into a clean, hot jar.
The vinegar may be stored in a cool, dark place for up to 2 months. Refrigerate it for longer storage.
MAKES 2½ CUPS

VINEGAR VARIATIONS

Vinegars are the quickest and least expensive gifts to make. Begin with red, white, wine or cider vinegar, add fresh or dried herbs or a combination of herbs or fresh or frozen fruit such as citrus or berries. Bring to a simmer on top of the stove or in a microwave. Store in a cool, dark place for at least 5 days and strain. Pour into clean bottles, preferably ones with small necks and shoulders to keep the herbs from floating to the top. For herb vinegars, insert wooden skewers with garlic, chilies, slices of lemon or orange, and sprigs of fresh herbs. Flavored vinegars make great nonfat salad dressings and can be used in marinades and sauces.

HERB VINEGAR

Almost any fresh herb or combination of herbs will enhance the flavor of vinegar. Experiment while they're in season.

2 cups white, cider, or wine vinegar
½ cup chopped fresh herbs, such as basil,
   rosemary, tarragon, thyme, oregano
3 to 4 whole cloves garlic (optional)
1 or 2 sprigs fresh herbs per bottle (optional)
1 whole red or green chili pepper per bottle
   (optional)

✳ Place the vinegar in a nonaluminum saucepan and bring to a boil. Place the chopped herbs in a clean glass jar. Add the garlic, if desired. Pour the hot vinegar over, cover, and place in a cool, dark place for 5 days, stirring once a day. Strain. Add the sprigs of fresh herbs and chili pepper for a zestier taste and garnish, if desired.
The vinegar may be stored in a cool, dark place for up to 2 months. Refrigerate it for longer storage.
MAKES 2 CUPS

HOW TO SEAL JAMS AND PRESERVES

I've never done much sterilizing and canning, although I enjoy incorporating homemade jams into gift baskets. I prefer to simply refrigerate or freeze the jam or preserves and include instructions with it so the recipient knows to do the same. Should you prefer to store jars at room temperature, it is important to can them properly. Sterilize jars and two-piece self-sealing lids. Ladle hot jam into hot jars. Leave ½ inch head space between the top of the jam and the jar lid. Wipe rims and threads clean. Top with lids and firmly screw on bands. Process in boiling water canner for five minutes if you live less than one thousand feet above sea level and for ten minutes if you live more than one thousand feet above sea level. Transfer the jars from the water to a towel and cool in a draft-free place for twelve to twenty-four hours. Test the seal to make sure it is secure. If the lid doesn't stay down, store the jar in the refrigerator.

STRAWBERRY-PINEAPPLE JAM

Pretty and pink, this jam is thin enough to double as an ice-cream topping.

1 package (10 ounces) frozen strawberries in syrup, defrosted
1 can (1 pound 4 ounces) crushed pineapple in its own syrup
4½ cups sugar
Grated peel and juice from 1 lemon
Grated peel and juice from 3 oranges
2 packages (3 ounces each) liquid pectin

❊ Place the strawberries and pineapple, with their syrup, in a deep, heavy saucepan. Stir in the sugar and the peel and juice from lemon and oranges. Cook over moderate heat, stirring occasionally, until the sugar is completely dissolved. Increase the heat to high, bring to a full rolling boil, and boil rapidly for 1 minute. Stir in the pectin and continue boiling rapidly for 4 minutes, stirring occasionally. Remove from the heat and stir for about 5 minutes to keep the fruit from falling to the bottom. Sterilize jam jars and lids by washing them carefully and placing them in boiling water to cover for 10 minutes. Spoon the jam into the still-hot jars and seal. Refrigerate for up to 2 months, or freeze for up to 1 year. For long-term storage, seal jars with two-part vacuum lids and process in a boiling water canner for 5 to 10 minutes (see first column, this page).

MAKES SIX 7-OUNCE JARS

APRICOT PRESERVES

The wonderfully intense flavor of dried apricots really comes through in this outstanding, thick jam.

1 pound dried apricots
1½ cups water
1 pound sugar

Simmer the apricots and water in a medium saucepan until soft, about 10 minutes. Remove the apricots with a slotted spoon to a food processor fitted with the metal blade. Puree until smooth, then return them to the water in the saucepan. Stir in the sugar and cook slowly over moderately low heat, stirring occasionally, until the mixture is thick, about 40 minutes. Sterilize jam jars and lids by washing them carefully and placing them in boiling water to cover for 10 minutes. Spoon the jam into the still-hot jars and seal. Refrigerate for up to 2 months, or freeze for up to 1 year. For long-term storage, seal jars with two-part vacuum lids and process in a boiling water canner for 5 to 10 minutes (see first column, this page).

MAKES FIVE 8-OUNCE JARS

BLUEBERRY-APPLE JAM

When summer has past and fresh blueberries are gone, make this blue ribbon cinnamon-scented jam with frozen berries.

4 cups sugar
2 tablespoons water
2 teaspoons ground cinnamon
2 teaspoons lemon juice
2 bags (1 pound each) frozen blueberries, defrosted
1 pound (about 2) green apples, peeled, halved, cored, and chopped

Stir the sugar, water, cinnamon, lemon juice, and blueberries in a 6-quart saucepan. Bring to a boil over moderate heat, stirring occasionally. Stir in the apples. Insert a candy thermometer and cook, stirring, over moderately high heat until the thermometer reaches 212 degrees, about 15 minutes. Sterilize jam jars and lids by washing them carefully and placing them in boiling water to cover for 10 minutes. Spoon the jam into the still-hot jars and seal. Refrigerate for up to 2 months, or freeze for up to 1 year. For long-term storage, seal jars with two-part vacuum lids and process in a boiling water canner for 5 to 10 minutes (see page 18).

MAKES ABOUT SIX 8-OUNCE JARS

CRANBERRY CHUTNEY

Introduce a new flavor to your curry dinners or serve this as an accompaniment to roast turkey, chicken, ham, or pork.

1½ cups white vinegar
1½ cups packed light brown sugar
½ cup candied ginger, chopped
1½ teaspoons chili powder
1 tablespoon mustard seeds
½ teaspoon ground cloves
1 teaspoon salt
1 cup raisins
1 clove garlic, finely minced
1 onion, chopped
1 can (20 ounces) crushed pineapple, undrained
1 can (16 ounces) whole-berry cranberry sauce

✸ Combine the vinegar, brown sugar, ginger, chili powder, mustard seeds, cloves, salt, raisins, garlic, onion, and pineapple in a heavy, medium-sized nonaluminum saucepan. Bring to a boil over moderate heat, stirring

occasionally to prevent scorching. Cook at a slow boil, uncovered, for 45 minutes, stirring occasionally. Add the cranberry sauce and cook 15 minutes longer. Sterilize jam jars and lids by washing them carefully and placing them in boiling water to cover for 10 minutes. Spoon the jam into the still-hot jars and seal. Refrigerate for up to 2 months, or freeze for up to 1 year. For long-term storage, seal jars with two-part vacuum lids and process in a boiling water canner for 5 to 10 minutes (see page 18).

MAKES 5 CUPS

TARRAGON MUSTARD

Replace fancy "gourmet" mustards with this easy-to-prepare, superior, and less expensive one.

½ cup dry mustard
½ cup red wine vinegar
½ cup sugar
2 large eggs, at room temperature
2 teaspoons dried tarragon, crumbled

✸ Mix the mustard and vinegar in a small nonaluminum saucepan; let sit 10 minutes for the mustard to dissolve. Whisk in the sugar, eggs, and tarragon. Cook over moderate heat, whisking constantly, until the mixture thickens and is very hot to the touch. Do not boil. Immediately remove to a bowl or glass jar and cool to room temperature.

The mustard may be tightly covered and kept in the refrigerator for several months.

MAKES 1⅓ CUPS

REFRIGERATOR PICKLES

Cold and crunchy, these will last a long time in your refrigerator—if you can resist helping yourself. Don't just think of them as pickles; they also make a splendid salad.

3 hothouse (long, thin) cucumbers, unpeeled, or 4 regular cucumbers, peeled (about 3½ pounds)
1¼ teaspoons salt
1 large green bell pepper, seeded and chopped
1 yellow onion, sliced thin
1 cup white vinegar
1¼ cups sugar
2 teaspoons celery seeds

✸ Slice the cucumbers into ¼-inch slices by hand or in a food processor with the medium slicing blade. Mix the slices with salt in a colander in the sink; let stand 2 hours. Drain the cucumbers well and place in a large bowl. Stir in the bell pepper and onion. Stir the vinegar, sugar, and celery seeds in a small bowl, until the sugar is dissolved. Pour over the vegetables. Refrigerate, covered, for at least 24 hours before serving.

The pickles may be refrigerated for up to 1 month.

MAKES ABOUT 9 CUPS

GIVING THANKS

Hands

    Joined together

Around the table.

    Callused hands

Ringed hands

    Tiny hands

Gnarled hands

Clasped together

    Young and old

In gratitude

    For family

And feast

    For harmony

And peace

    Fingers laced

With love

    In thankfulness

And prayer.

Marlene Sorosky

HAVE you ever stopped to think why Thanksgiving is so special? It's the only holiday where the singular focus is food—food enhanced only by family and loved ones. It's a meal where little tots sit next to grandmas and grandpas, spanning several generations. The air has become crisp and cool, and those leaves left on the trees are still autumn hued. It's the first holiday for which students who are away at school return home. So traditional are the foods of this celebration that the day is recognizable solely by the smells emanating from the kitchen. In order for you to truly enjoy the feast, my menu includes a selection of dishes which can be made ahead. They are practical, imaginative, and portable, and filled with traditional American flavors.

ROAST TURKEY WITH GIBLET GRAVY

How to Roast a Turkey

❊ Whenever possible, purchase a fresh turkey rather than a frozen one. Allow approximately 1 pound of turkey per average serving. Bring the turkey to room temperature several hours before cooking. Remove the giblets and any fat from inside the turkey cavity. Check the neck cavity for extra parts and remove them. Rinse and pat dry. Sprinkle salt and pepper into the cavities. Rub the skin all over with oil, salt or seasoned salt, and pepper. Lightly spoon the stuffing into the neck cavity and skewer the skin flap over. Stuff body cavity and skewer it closed with turkey lacers or a trussing needle. Tie the legs together or refasten with clamp, if provided. Place the turkey on a rack in a shallow roasting pan. If it is not too heavy to turn, begin it breast-side down. This allows the juices to accumulate in the breast and it will be juicier. To roast breast down, you need a rack that is shaped like a V. Add 1 cup chicken broth or water to the pan. Bake the turkey at 325 degrees for approximately 15 minutes per pound for a bird up to 16 pounds. Add 12 minutes per pound for each pound over 16. Baste occasionally with the pan juices. If cooking breast side down, turn breast up halfway through the roasting time. If the top gets too brown, cover it lightly with a tent of foil. Two-thirds through the roasting time, untie the drumsticks so the heat can reach the cavity. When you think the turkey is almost done, insert an instant-read thermometer into the thickest part of the thigh, but not touching the bone. It should read 180 degrees for the dark meat, 170 degrees for the white meat. Remove the turkey to a carving board and let it rest at least 20 minutes before carving. A cooked turkey will stay warm for 1 to 2 hours before it is carved.

How to Make Giblet Stock for Gravy

Turkey giblets and neck
1 large onion, sliced (about 1 cup)
¼ cup celery leaves
½ cup sliced carrots
1 cup dry white wine
3 cups chicken broth

❊ Cut the turkey neck and heart in half. If using the liver, refrigerate until you are ready to use it. Place the giblets in a medium saucepan. Add the onion, celery leaves, carrots, wine, and chicken broth. Bring the mixture to a boil, lower the heat, and simmer, partially covered, for 2 to 2½ hours, or until the gizzard is tender. If using the liver, add it the last half hour. Strain, pressing on the vegetables; reserve the broth. Chop the giblets, the meat from the neck, and the liver if using. Refrigerate broth and meat separately.

How to Make Gravy

Drippings from cooked turkey
Giblet stock (recipe above) or chicken broth
Instant-blending or all-purpose flour
Reserved cooked giblets (optional)
Salt and pepper

❊ When the turkey is done (or about 15 minutes before, if desired) pour the drippings from the roasting pan into a pitcher or gravy separator. If using a pitcher, place it in the freezer for 10 to 15 minutes, or until the fat rises to the top. Skim off the fat. For each cup of gravy desired, measure 1 tablespoon of fat back into the roasting pan. Stir in 1 tablespoon flour for each tablespoon fat. Cook, stirring occasionally, over low heat, scraping up brown bits from the bottom of the pan, until the mixture is golden. Slowly whisk in the drippings and enough giblet stock or chicken broth to make 1 cup. Bring to a boil, stirring and scraping up all brown bits from the bottom of the pan. Stir in the chopped giblets and liver, if desired. Simmer 5 minutes. Season to taste with salt and pepper.

How to Carve a Turkey

❊ Place the turkey on a cutting board. Cut off the wings. Remove each leg including the thigh, by carving between the breast and the leg, cutting all the way down to the thigh bone; twist loose at the thigh socket. Separate the drumstick and thigh by cutting between the bones. Slice the leg and thigh meat. Remove each breast half by cutting down next to the breast bone and scraping the meat away from the bone, removing each breast in one piece. Slice the breast meat. Scrape off any remaining meat with the knife.

How to Bake Stuffing in a Casserole Dish

❋ Stuffing may be baked either in a casserole dish or in the cavity of a bird. Often a recipe yields enough for both. Technically, when it is baked in a casserole dish, it is called a dressing. A stuffing that bakes in the cavity gets the benefit of the turkey's juices. When baking in a casserole dish, add extra liquid, so the dressing will remain moist. The liquid can be giblet stock, chicken broth, or wine. Grease a casserole dish and fill with the dressing. Cover with a lid or foil.

❋ Stuffing may be refrigerated overnight, if desired. Bring to room temperature and bake at 325 or 350 degrees (you might want to put it in the same oven with the turkey). Bake for 30 to 45 minutes; uncover and bake 30 minutes longer, or until the top is crisp. If desired, baste with turkey drippings and stir once or twice during the last 30 minutes.

To make a fall centerpiece, arrange a variety of breads, rolls, and bread sticks in a low basket. Intersperse them with fresh and dried flowers and wheat.

CRANBERRY-APPLE STUFFING

I prefer making stuffing with fresh bread rather than packaged stuffing mix. That way I can season it to my taste. Here crumbled egg bread is tossed with apples, cranberry sauce, raisins, and dried apricots for an extremely flavorful, fruity mixture.

1 package (16 ounces) sliced egg bread
¼ pound (1 stick) butter or margarine
1 cup chopped onion (about 1 large onion)
1 cup chopped celery (about 2 stalks)
¼ cup (about 1 ounce) chopped dried apricots
2 cups (about 2 medium) peeled and diced green apples, such as pippin or Granny Smith
1 cup (about 4 ounces) chopped walnuts
½ cup golden raisins
1 can (16 ounces) whole-berry cranberry sauce
½ teaspoon dried thyme
½ teaspoon dried savory (optional)
2 teaspoons salt, or to taste
4 large eggs, lightly beaten

❋ Preheat the oven to 325 degrees.

❋ Tear the bread into pieces and place several handfuls at a time in a food processor fitted with the metal blade. Process on and off until you have coarse crumbs. Remove the crumbs to a shallow roasting pan and continue processing the remaining bread. Bake the crumbs for 30 to 40 minutes, stirring every 10 minutes, until they are lightly browned and toasted. Remove from the oven and cool to room temperature.

❋ Meanwhile, melt the butter or margarine in a large skillet and sauté the onion and celery until soft. Stir the onion-celery mixture into the crumbs, using your hands or a large spoon. Mix in the apricots, apples, nuts, raisins, cranberry sauce, thyme, savory (if using), salt, and eggs.

The stuffing may be refrigerated overnight.

❋ Stuff the cavity of a turkey or bake in a casserole dish.

MAKES ENOUGH STUFFING FOR A 16-POUND TURKEY

Leaner: Substitute 3 tablespoons olive oil for the butter. If stuffing is too dry, moisten with some broth.

CORN BREAD-SAUSAGE STUFFING

Making corn bread from a mix takes only minutes, but your stuffing will be so far superior to those using a prepackaged stuffing that it's well worth the time. By toasting the bread in the oven, the stuffing retains some of its crunch even after cooking in the turkey's cavity.

1 package (16 ounces) corn bread mix
1 package (12 ounces) bulk pork sausage
¼ pound (1 stick) butter or margarine
1 cup chopped celery (about 2 stalks)
1 cup chopped onion (about 1 large onion)
1 teaspoon dried thyme
1 teaspoon dried sage
1 cup chopped fresh parsley leaves
1 cup giblet stock (page 24) or chicken broth
Salt and pepper

❋ Preheat the oven as directed on corn bread package. Make corn bread as directed. Let cool slightly, break it into 1-inch chunks. Place the chunks on a baking sheet and bake for 30 minutes, or until toasted, stirring every 10 minutes. Remove the corn bread from the oven and cool to room temperature.

The corn bread may be prepared 2 days ahead.

❋ Meanwhile, cook the sausage in a large skillet over moderately high heat until browned, breaking it up with a fork while browning. Remove the sausage with a slotted spoon and place it in a large bowl. Discard all but 2 tablespoons of the drippings. Melt the butter in the drippings; sauté the celery and onion until soft. Stir in the thyme, sage, and parsley.

The mixtures may be refrigerated in separate containers for up to 2 days.

❋ Before using, stir the corn bread and cooked onion-celery mixture into the sausage. Add the stock or broth and mix lightly but thoroughly with your hands or a large spoon. Add salt and pepper to taste. Stuff the cavity of a turkey or bake the stuffing in a casserole dish.

MAKES ENOUGH STUFFING FOR 13- TO
16-POUND TURKEY

Leaner: Substitute 3 tablespoons vegetable oil for the butter. If too dry, moisten with additional broth.

To make a bread stick place card, break four bread sticks into various sizes. Hold them in place with a rubber band. Tie raffia or ribbon around the rubber band. To stand it up, insert broken toothpicks into the bottom of two of the bread sticks and attach them to a leaf or a slice of party rye or pumpernickel. Decorate with a sprig of wheat or dried or fresh flowers.

ORANGE-CRANBERRY-APPLE RELISH

As soon as cranberries are available, prepare this fresh, no-cook relish in your food processor. It keeps in the refrigerator for months and makes terrific gifts.

1 package (12 ounces) fresh cranberries
2 medium pippin or Granny Smith apples, peeled, quartered, and cored (about 2 cups)
¾ cup sugar
½ cup orange marmalade
2 teaspoons lemon juice
2 teaspoons Grand Marnier
1½ cups (about 6 ounces) chopped walnuts
⅛ teaspoon ground cinnamon

❋ Chop the cranberries fine in a food processor fitted with the metal blade. Remove to a large bowl. Chop the apples in the food processor; add them to the cranberries. Stir in the sugar, marmalade, lemon juice, Grand Marnier, nuts, and cinnamon. Cover tightly and refrigerate overnight before serving.
The relish may be refrigerated for up to 2 months.

MAKES ABOUT 5 CUPS

GINGERSNAP-YAM PUDDING

The sugar and spice in crushed gingersnap cookies form a flavorful crust for yams. Eggs whipped into the yams turn them into a custard that cuts into perfect squares.

30 gingersnap cookies
1 large can (2 pounds 8 ounces) plus one small can (1 pound 13 ounces) yams, drained
3 large eggs
1 teaspoon salt
½ teaspoon ground cinnamon
¼ teaspoon ground nutmeg
¼ teaspoon ground allspice
¼ cup sugar
Grated peel of 1 orange
1 cup half-and-half
1 cup orange juice
2 tablespoons lemon juice
2 tablespoons butter or margarine, at room temperature

❋ Preheat the oven to 325 degrees. Grease or spray a 9 x 13-inch glass baking dish. Crush the gingersnaps in a food processor fitted with the metal blade or with a rolling pin until they are in fine crumbs. Reserve ½ cup crumbs for topping. Press the remaining crumbs over the bottom of the baking dish.

❋ Mix the yams in a large bowl with an electric mixer at medium speed until fluffy, about 2 minutes. Add the eggs, one at a time, mixing well after each. Mix in the salt, cinnamon, nutmeg, allspice, sugar, and orange peel. Reduce the mixer to low speed and slowly pour in half-and-half and orange and lemon juices, mixing until incorporated. Pour the mixture over the crumbs, smoothing the top. Sprinkle with the reserved ½ cup crumbs. Dot with butter.

❋ Bake the pudding, uncovered, in the center of the oven for 1 hour, or until it is puffed and golden. A knife inserted in the center should come out clean. Let the pudding rest 20 minutes. Cut it into squares to serve.
The pudding may be refrigerated or frozen after it is baked. Cool it to room temperature, cover, and refrigerate or freeze. Before serving, bring it to room temperature and bake at 350 degrees for 30 minutes, or until heated through.

SERVES 12 TO 14

Leaner: Substitute 1 cup whole milk for the half-and-half. Substitute 4 egg whites for 2 of the whole eggs. Omit the butter.

ZUCCHINI-RICE CASSEROLE

Here's an example of successfully reducing fat and increasing flavor in a recipe. I used to make this casserole with more than a pint of cream and twice as much cheese. It is so delicious now, I wouldn't dream of making it any other way.

2 pounds zucchini, ends trimmed
2 tablespoons olive oil
1 large onion, chopped
4 large cloves garlic, finely chopped
2 tablespoons all-purpose flour

2 ½ cups whole or low-fat milk
½ cup uncooked long-grain white rice
¾ cup Parmesan cheese
1 teaspoon dried basil
1 teaspoon dried thyme
1 cup regular, low-fat, or nonfat mozzarella
    cheese, cut into small cubes
1 teaspoon salt, or to taste
Pepper

✳ Preheat the oven to 425 degrees. Grease or spray a 9 x 13-inch glass baking dish.

✳ Shred the zucchini. Heat the oil in a large skillet over high heat. Sauté the onion until golden, about 10 minutes. Stir in the garlic and shredded zucchini. Cook over moderately high heat for 5 minutes, stirring constantly, until zucchini begins to wilt. Sprinkle with the flour and cook, stirring, until the flour is absorbed. Stir in the milk, rice, ½ cup of the Parmesan cheese, basil, thyme, mozzarella, salt, and pepper to taste. Pour into prepared casserole dish. Sprinkle top with remaining ¼ cup Parmesan cheese.

✳ Bake, uncovered, for 30 to 40 minutes, or until golden and most of the liquid has evaporated. Remove from the oven and let sit for 10 to 20 minutes before serving.

The casserole may be well covered and refrigerated overnight. Reheat it at 375 degrees for 15 minutes, or until heated through and bubbling.
SERVES 12

Let us give thanks before we turn
To other things of less concern
For all the poetry of the table.
Louis Untermeyer

BROCCOLI-ONION CASSEROLE

Broccoli spears and baby onions bake in a delicately flavored cheese sauce.

3 packages (10 ounces each) frozen broccoli
    spears, defrosted
4 tablespoons (½ stick) butter or margarine
¼ cup all-purpose flour
2 cups whole or low-fat milk
1 teaspoon dry mustard
1 teaspoon Dijon-style mustard
¾ teaspoon salt, or to taste
½ teaspoon freshly ground pepper, or to taste
1 ½ cups (about 6 ounces) shredded sharp
    regular or low-fat Cheddar cheese
½ cup grated Parmesan cheese
1 package (1 pound) frozen small whole
    onions, not defrosted
1 cup fresh bread crumbs (about 3 slices
    day-old bread, crusts removed)
2 tablespoons butter or margarine, melted

✳ Cut 1 to 1 ½ inches off the ends of the broccoli spears and discard. Place the broccoli on paper towels and dry as thoroughly as possible. Melt butter in a medium saucepan. Stir in the flour and cook over low heat, stirring for 1 minute. Slowly stir in the milk, whisking constantly over moderate heat until the mixture comes to a boil and thickens. Whisk in the dry and Dijon mustards, salt, and pepper. Remove the sauce from the heat and stir in the Cheddar and Parmesan cheeses. Taste and adjust the seasonings, if necessary.

✳ Place the broccoli in the bottom of a 9 x 13-inch casserole dish. Scatter the onions over the top. Spoon the cheese sauce over the onions, spreading it to cover as evenly as possible. Stir the bread crumbs with the melted butter in a small bowl; sprinkle them over the top.

The casserole may be covered with plastic wrap and refrigerated overnight.

✳ Preheat the oven to 400 degrees. Bake, uncovered, for 25 to 30 minutes, or until the broccoli spears are tender when pierced with the tip of a small knife. Adjust the broiler to the highest setting. Broil the casserole for 2 to 3 minutes, or until the crumbs are golden.
SERVES 8 TO 10

PUMPKIN-MOLASSES MUFFINS

For a real taste treat, slather these dark, moist, velvety muffins with a sprightly ginger-flavored butter.

¼ pound (1 stick) butter or margarine,
    at room temperature
¾ cup packed light brown sugar
1 large egg
1 cup canned pumpkin
¼ cup molasses
1 ¾ cups all-purpose flour
1 teaspoon baking soda
¾ teaspoon ground ginger
¼ teaspoon salt
¼ cup finely chopped pecans
Ginger-Honey Butter, for serving
    (optional; recipe follows)

✳ Preheat the oven to 375 degrees. Grease 18 two-inch muffin cups. In a food processor fitted with the metal blade or in a medium-sized mixing bowl, cream the butter and brown sugar until well blended. Add the egg, pumpkin, and molasses, mixing well. The mixture will be grainy. Add the flour, baking soda, ginger, and salt, mixing until they are incorporated. Mix in the pecans. Spoon the batter into the muffin cups, filling them half full. Bake for 15 minutes, or until the tops are puffed and spring back when lightly pressed with the fingertips.

The muffins may wrapped airtight and frozen. Defrost them, wrapped, at room temperature. Reheat at 350 degrees for 5 minutes, or until they are heated through.

❋ Serve warm with Ginger-Honey Butter, if desired.

MAKES 18 MUFFINS

Ginger-Honey Butter
6 tablespoons (¾ stick) butter or margarine, at room temperature
2 tablespoons honey
½ teaspoon ground ginger

❋ In a small bowl, cream the butter and stir in the honey and ginger until blended. Spoon the mixture into a serving bowl or make butter molds by spreading the butter into chocolate molds. Freeze the butter until solid; pop out. Store in the refrigerator up to 2 days or freeze. Bring to room temperature 15 minutes before serving.

MAKES ABOUT ½ CUP

NOT HOSTING
THANKSGIVING?
Many recipes in this menu travel well. Both vegetable casseroles and the yam pudding are assembled, baked, and served in one dish. Pumpkin-Molasses Muffins with Ginger-Honey Butter would make a unique addition to a friend's menu. If oven space is not available, choose the cranberry relish.

A SMALL BOUNTY
FOR FOUR
ORANGE-CHUTNEY GLAZED CORNISH HENS WITH WHITE AND WILD RICE STUFFING

ROASTED RED BELL PEPPER, ZUCCHINI, AND SPINACH SALAD

SNOW PEAS WITH WATER CHESTNUTS

HERBED BISCUITS

A SELECTED PIE
(SEE PAGES 32-35)

ORANGE-CHUTNEY GLAZED CORNISH HENS WITH WHITE AND WILD RICE STUFFING
Filled with succulent rice enhanced with chutney, apples, and peanuts, these beautiful hens are glazed with an orange sauce that turns them a deep, rich, chestnut brown. This recipe yields enough stuffing for 5 hens.

4 Cornish game hens (about 1¼ pounds each)
Salt and pepper
1 package (6 ounces) long-grain white and wild rice
½ cup peeled, diced cooking apple (pippin or Granny Smith) (about ½ apple)
¼ cup coarsely chopped salted peanuts
1 jar (12 ounces) chutney, chopped
½ teaspoon ground ginger
¼ teaspoon poultry seasoning
3 tablespoons currants or chopped raisins
3 tablespoons butter or margarine, melted
½ cup orange juice
2 teaspoons cider vinegar
¼ cup dry red wine

❋ Remove the hens from their wrappings; remove the giblets and save for another use. Dry the hens well. Sprinkle salt and pepper into the cavities. Prepare the rice according to directions on the package. Cool to room temperature. Stir in the apple, peanuts, 2 heaping tablespoons of the chutney, ginger, poultry seasoning, and currants or raisins. Spoon the stuffing into the cavities of the hens. You will have a little left over. (Bake it separately in a baking dish.) Tie the legs together with string.

❋ Preheat the oven to 400 degrees. Brush the tops of the hens with melted butter and sprinkle with salt and pepper. Place the hens on a rack in a shallow roasting pan. Bake for 30 minutes.

❋ Make the glaze by combining the orange juice, remaining chutney, and vinegar in a small saucepan. After the hens have baked 30 minutes, reduce the oven temperature to 350 degrees and continue baking for 15 minutes. Brush the hens with the orange glaze. Continue to bake 45 minutes longer, brushing with glaze every 10 minutes. The hens should roast approximately 1½ hours, or until very well browned and glazed. Remove the hens from the oven and let rest 15 minutes before serving.

❋ Meanwhile, add wine to the remaining glaze in the saucepan. Simmer slowly until the mixture is reduced slightly. Season with salt and pepper and serve with the hens.

SERVES 4

ROASTED RED BELL PEPPER, ZUCCHINI, AND SPINACH SALAD
This exceptionally colorful and refreshing salad is made with marinated strips of red bell pepper and rounds of zucchini tossed with bright green spinach leaves.

Italian Vinaigrette

3 tablespoons chicken or vegetable broth

2 tablespoons balsamic vinegar

2 tablespoons fresh lemon juice,
    plus more to taste

1 medium clove garlic, minced

¼ cup olive oil

¼ cup regular, low-fat, or nonfat plain yogurt

Salt and pepper

Salad

1 pound zucchini, thinly sliced
    (about 2 medium)

½ cup sliced green onions

3 red bell peppers

6 ounces (about 4 cups) cleaned and
    stemmed spinach

✳ To make the Italian vinaigrette, in a medium bowl, whisk together broth, vinegar, 2 tablespoons of the lemon juice and garlic. Whisk in oil and yogurt until thoroughly blended. Do not use food processor—it will break down the yogurt. Season with salt and pepper and additional lemon juice, to taste.

The vinaigrette may be refrigerated for up to 3 days. It will thicken as it sits. Shake or stir it well before using.

✳ To roast the peppers, preheat the broiler to its highest setting. Line the broiler rack with foil and place it so the tops of the peppers are about 4 inches from the heat. Broil the peppers, turning them on all sides, until their skins are charred. Wrap the peppers in a kitchen towel or paper bag to steam for 10 minutes. Transfer them to a colander and rinse under cold running water until cool enough to handle. Peel the skins off under the running water. Cut out the core and seeds and slice the flesh into strips.

The peppers may be covered and refrigerated overnight.

✳ Three to four hours before serving the salad, place the zucchini and green onions in a medium bowl. Pour the vinaigrette over the vegetables, cover, and marinate in the refrigerator. About 2 hours before serving, add the peppers to the zucchini mixture, and refrigerate.

✳ Before serving, put the spinach in a large bowl, add the vegetables with as much vinaigrette as desired, and toss well.

SERVES 4 TO 6

Faster: Substitute one 7-ounce jar roasted red bell peppers, drained and patted dry, for the fresh ones.

SNOW PEAS WITH WATER CHESTNUTS

This simple vegetable dish enhances any meat or fish served with a sauce. If fresh snow peas are available, they are preferable, but frozen work well, too.

½ pound fresh snow peas or 2 packages
    (6 ounces each) frozen snow peas

1 tablespoon butter or margarine

½ an 8-ounce can (4 ounces) water chestnuts,
    drained and sliced

1 clove garlic, finely minced

½ teaspoon salt, or to taste

½ teaspoon pepper

½ teaspoon lemon juice

✳ Wash fresh snow peas, if using; trim the ends and string. Defrost frozen snow peas and drain on paper towels. Melt the butter or margarine in a wok or large skillet. Add the snow peas, water chestnuts, garlic, salt, pepper, and lemon juice. Cook over high heat, stirring, until the vegetables are tender but still crunchy. Serve immediately.

SERVES 4

HERBED BISCUITS

Packaged refrigerated biscuits take on a new look when they are cut into bite-sized pieces, rolled in herbed garlic butter, and baked in a cake pan. So easy and so good.

4 tablespoons (½ stick) butter or margarine

1 package (10 ounces) refrigerated biscuits

2 cloves garlic, finely chopped

1 heaping tablespoon chopped fresh parsley

1 teaspoon dried basil

½ teaspoon dried oregano

½ teaspoon dried thyme

2 tablespoons grated Parmesan cheese

1 tablespoon sesame seeds

✳ Preheat the oven to 400 degrees. Place the oven rack in the lower third of the oven. Put the butter in a 9-inch cake pan and place in the oven for 3 to 5 minutes, until melted. Separate the biscuits and cut each into 4 pieces. Stir the garlic into the butter. Sprinkle the parsley, basil, oregano, thyme, Parmesan cheese, and sesame seeds over the butter; stir lightly. Arrange the pieces of biscuit next to each other in the butter.

The pan of biscuits may be covered and refrigerated for several hours. Bring it to room temperature 1 hour before baking.

✳ Bake for 12 to 17 minutes, or until the tops are very brown. Immediately invert the biscuits onto a serving plate and serve.

SERVES 4 TO 6

FLAKY PASTRY

This recipe has long been my favorite all-purpose pie crust. The butter adds flavor, the shortening, flakiness. If you wish to make pastry for a double-crust pie, follow the directions, doubling the ingredients.

1¼ cups all-purpose flour

¼ teaspoon salt

¼ pound (1 stick) cold unsalted butter,
    cut into 16 pieces

2 tablespoons vegetable shortening,
    chilled in freezer

3 to 5 tablespoons ice water

✻ Place the flour and salt in a food processor fitted with the metal blade or in a mixing bowl. Add the butter and shortening and pulse 6 to 8 times in the food processor or mix with a pastry blender or two forks until pieces are the size of peas. Add 3 tablespoons of the ice water and mix until the flour is moistened. If the dough is too crumbly, add additional water, a teaspoon at a time, until the dough holds together. Do not continue mixing until a ball forms, but rather wrap the moistened dough in plastic wrap, shape it into a ball, and flatten it into a disk. Refrigerate the dough until cold enough to roll.

The pastry may be well wrapped and refrigerated for up to 2 days, or it may be frozen. Defrost it at room temperature until soft enough to roll, but still very cold.
MAKES PASTRY FOR ONE 9-INCH PIE OR
ONE 11-INCH TART

HARD TO ROLL?
If pastry sticks to the rolling pin, chill the rolling pin in the freezer.

NEW ENGLAND PUMPKIN PIE

If you are not inclined to make your own pie crust, this custard filling will fit into a frozen 9-inch deep-dish pie shell. If you buy a 29-ounce can of pumpkin for this pie, you will have 1 cup of pumpkin left over—just the amount needed to make the Pumpkin-Molasses Muffins (page 28–29).

1 recipe Flaky Pastry (this page)

3 large eggs

2 cups canned pumpkin

½ cup packed light brown sugar

½ cup granulated sugar

1 teaspoon ground cinnamon

½ teaspoon ground ginger

½ teaspoon salt

¼ teaspoon ground nutmeg

¼ teaspoon ground cloves

1¼ cups whole or low-fat evaporated milk
    (from a 12-ounce can)

1 cup whipping cream whipped with 2 table-
    spoons powdered sugar, if desired

✻ Make Flaky Pastry as directed.
✻ Preheat the oven to 350 degrees. Place a rack in the lower third of the oven. Roll out the pastry on a lightly floured surface and fit it into

a 9-or 10-inch pie dish. Trim the edges 1 inch larger than the dish. Fold the dough under to make a raised rim, and flute the edges.
✻ To make filling, whisk the eggs lightly in a large bowl. Add the pumpkin, brown and granulated sugars, cinnamon, ginger, salt, nutmeg, and cloves, whisking until well combined. Gradually whisk in the milk. Pour the mixture into the prepared shell. Bake for 60 to 70 minutes, or until a knife inserted in the center comes out with just a small amount of custard adhering to it. Remove the pie to a rack and cool.
The pie may be covered with foil and refrigerated for up to 2 days, or it may be frozen. Defrost it, covered, at room temperature. To serve warm, uncover and reheat at 350 degrees for 10 minutes, or until hot.
✻ Serve warm or chilled. Pass sweetened whipped cream to spoon over each piece when serving, if desired.
SERVES 6 TO 8

PUMPKIN-PRALINE CHEESE TART

With its pumpkin cheesecake filling and crunchy toffee-nut glaze, this pie can stand proudly beside your traditional one.

1 recipe Flaky Pastry (this page)

Pumpkin Cheese Filling

2 packages (3 ounces each) regular, low-fat, or
    nonfat cream cheese, at room temperature

¾ cup packed light brown sugar

1 teaspoon ground cinnamon

¼ teaspoon ground ginger

Cranberry Cream Pie, page 34

½ teaspoon ground nutmeg

¼ teaspoon salt

2 large eggs, at room temperature

1 cup canned pumpkin

1 cup regular or low-fat sour cream

1 teaspoon vanilla extract

Praline Topping

1½ cups (about 6 ounces) chopped pecans

¾ cup packed light brown sugar

4 tablespoons (½ stick) butter, melted

✹ Make Flaky Pastry as directed.

✹ Preheat the oven to 475 degrees. Place a rack in the lower third of the oven. Roll the pastry on a lightly floured surface to a 13-inch circle approximately ¼ inch thick. Drape the pastry over an 11-inch tart pan with a removable bottom, pressing it into the bottom and sides. Fold the excess pastry inside itself to reinforce the sides. Cover the pastry with aluminum foil and fill it with pie weights or dried beans even with the rim of the pan. Bake it for 15 minutes. Carefully remove the foil and weights and continue to bake for 6 to 8 minutes, or until the pastry is golden. Remove to a rack and cool to room temperature.

The crust may be covered and kept at room temperature overnight, or may be wrapped and frozen.

✹ Reduce the oven heat to 375 degrees. To make the filling, place the cream cheese, brown sugar, cinnamon, ginger, nutmeg, and salt in a large mixing bowl. With a mixer at medium speed, blend until creamy. Add the eggs one at a time, beating well after each. Add the pumpkin, sour cream, and vanilla extract, mixing until smooth and blended. Pour the filling

into the baked crust and bake at 375 degrees for 45 to 50 minutes, or until the tip of a knife inserted near the center comes out clean. Cool to room temperature.

The tart may be covered with foil and refrigerated overnight, or frozen. Defrost it, covered, at room temperature.

✹ Before serving, or up to 4 hours ahead, make the praline topping by mixing nuts, brown sugar, and melted butter together with a fork in a small bowl. Sprinkle evenly over the top of the tart. Broil under high heat until the sugar is melted and bubbling, 2 to 4 minutes. Watch carefully, as it burns quickly. Leave at room temperature until ready to serve.

SERVES 8

It's easier to work with dough that is too cold than too warm. It takes a little extra muscle to roll it, which is far more desirable than having it stick.

CRANBERRY CREAM PIE

Cranberries need not be limited to sauces. Their intense color and flavor spread over a creamy no-bake filling makes a spectacular pie.

Crust

1¼ cups graham cracker crumbs

2 tablespoons sugar

⅓ cup chopped pecans

6 tablespoons (¾ stick) butter or margarine, melted

Cream Cheese Filling

1 package (8 ounces) regular or low-fat cream cheese, at room temperature

⅓ cup powdered sugar

1 teaspoon vanilla extract

2 tablespoons Grand Marnier

1 cup whipping cream

Cranberry Topping

1 cup sugar

3 tablespoons water

2½ cups cranberries

2 heaping tablespoons cornstarch

To make the crust, preheat the oven to 350 degrees. Place the crumbs, sugar, nuts, and melted butter in a mixing bowl or a food processor fitted with the metal blade and mix them until combined. Press the mixture onto the bottom and sides of a 9-inch pie dish or 11-inch tart pan. Bake the crust 8 to 10 minutes, or until lightly browned. Cool to room temperature.

✹ To make the filling, mix the cream cheese and powdered sugar in a small mixing bowl with electric mixer on medium speed until light and fluffy, about 3 minutes. Scrape the sides of the bowl and mix in vanilla extract and Grand Marnier. In a separate bowl, beat the whipping cream until soft peaks form. Fold it into the cream cheese mixture. Spoon the filling into the cooled crust, spreading evenly. Refrigerate several hours, or until well chilled.

The pie may be covered with foil and refrigerated overnight, or frozen.

✹ To make the topping, cook the sugar, 1 tablespoon of the water, and the cranberries in a medium saucepan, stirring constantly, until the mixture comes to a full boil and the berries begin to pop. Remove the pan from the heat. Dissolve the cornstarch in the remaining 2 tablespoons water; stir it into the cranberries. Return the pan to the heat and cook, stirring constantly, until the mixture comes to a boil and thickens. Remove it from the heat and cool to room temperature. Spread it over the cream cheese layer. Cover with plastic wrap and refrigerate until serving time or overnight.

SERVES 6 TO 8

CARAMEL APPLE TART

Before my daughter Caryn knew anything about cooking, she made this pie for a party. Her success convinces me that even the most novice cook will receive raves with this delectable mixture of caramel-soaked apples in a packaged puff pastry crust.

1 package (16 ounces) frozen puff pastry, defrosted until soft enough to roll, but still very cold

Caramel Sauce
1 cup sugar
½ cup water
¾ cup heavy whipping cream
3 tablespoons butter or margarine

Apple Filling
6 large tart cooking apples (about 3 pounds)
4 tablespoons (½ stick) butter or margarine
⅓ cup sugar
1 tablespoon all-purpose flour
1 egg lightly beaten with 1 teaspoon water, for glaze

✳ On a lightly floured surface, roll half the pastry (1 sheet) into a 13-inch square; transfer to an 11-inch tart pan with a removable bottom. Press pastry onto bottom and sides of pan; trim edges even with top rim. Refrigerate pastry-lined pan and remaining pastry while preparing the sauce and filling.

✳ To make the caramel sauce, combine sugar and water in a heavy medium-sized saucepan. Cook over moderately high heat, without stirring, until mixture turns golden brown; be careful not to let it burn. Immediately remove from heat and slowly stir in cream. The sugar will harden, but stirring will smooth it out. Stir in butter or margarine until melted.

✳ Place oven rack in lowest position. Preheat oven to 425 degrees. To make the apple filling, peel, halve, core, and thinly slice the apples. Heat butter or margarine in a large skillet over moderately high heat. Sauté apples, turning often, until barely tender, about 5 to 8 minutes. Remove from heat and sprinkle with sugar and flour, stirring until coated. Pour hot apples with their juices into pastry-lined pan.

✳ Measure ½ cup of the warm caramel sauce and pour over apples. (Reserve remaining sauce; it may be refrigerated up to 2 weeks. Reheat in microwave before serving.)

✳ Roll remaining pastry and cut a 12-inch circle; cut a 1-inch circle out of the center. Place over apples; press onto rim of pan and trim edges even with rim. Brush top lightly with egg glaze. If desired, reroll scraps of pastry, cut into decorations and place on top; brush with egg glaze.

✳ Place tart on baking sheet and bake for 30 to 40 minutes, or until deep golden brown. The top will have pulled away from the sides. Remove from oven and cool 10 minutes. To keep the sides from sticking, place the tart on a bowl smaller than the tart pan, carefully lower sides, then raise them back in place. Let the tart cool in the pan for at least 30 minutes before serving.

At this point, the tart may be covered and kept at room temperature overnight, or frozen. Before serving bring to room temperature and reheat, uncovered, at 425 degrees for 5 to 10 minutes, or until hot.

✳ To serve, remove sides of tart pan. Spoon warm sauce over each slice.

SERVES 8

THANKS FOR THE TURKEY (AGAIN)

TURKEY-VEGETABLE CHOWDER
PUFFED TURKEY SANDWICH LOAF
ORIENTAL TURKEY PASTA SALAD
THAI-INSPIRED TURKEY SALAD
TURKEY-RICE CASSEROLE

It isn't so much what's on the table that matters, as what's on the chairs.
W. S. Gilbert

TURKEY-VEGETABLE CHOWDER

Turning the leftover turkey carcass into a vegetable-laden soup is as much of a tradition in my house as cooking the turkey. Bacon adds a smoky flavor and no matter what vegetables you use, you'll never spoil it.

1 turkey carcass
10 cups cold water, or enough to barely cover turkey bones
1 tablespoon salt
1 whole onion, peeled and studded with 5 whole cloves
½ cup celery leaves
1 bay leaf
6 slices regular or reduced-fat bacon, chopped
2 carrots, peeled and sliced
2 onions, finely chopped
2 stalks celery, chopped
2 medium potatoes, peeled and cut into small cubes
1 can (16 ounces) whole tomatoes, undrained
1 package (10 ounces) frozen baby lima beans
1 package (10 ounces) frozen corn
2 cups chopped cooked turkey (bite-sized pieces)
1 cup whipping cream
¼ teaspoon cayenne pepper
Freshly ground black pepper
Chopped fresh parsley, for garnish

❋ To make turkey stock, place the carcass on a cutting board and cut into 8 to 10 pieces. Place the pieces in a soup pot with the water, salt, onion, celery leaves and bay leaf. Bring to a boil, lower the heat and simmer, covered, for 2 hours. Strain and set aside.

❋ Meanwhile, cook the bacon in a medium skillet until crisp. Remove and drain.

❋ Bring the strained stock to a boil. Add the bacon, carrots, onions, celery and potatoes. Simmer, uncovered, for 30 minutes, or until vegetables are tender. Chop the tomatoes and add them with their liquid, along with the lima beans, corn, and turkey, to the soup. Cook until heated through. Stir in the cream, cayenne, and black pepper to taste. Serve in soup bowls garnished with chopped parsley.
The soup may be refrigerated for up to 2 days, or frozen.
SERVES 6 TO 8

Leaner: Reduce the cream to ½ cup or substitute evaporated skim milk.

PUFFED TURKEY SANDWICH LOAF

This recipe gives the word "sandwich" new meaning. Scoop out half a loaf of French bread and fill it with slices of turkey and tomatoes. Spread it with a creamy, cheesy topping and broil until puffed and golden. It's hard to think of this as leftovers.

1 loaf (1 pound) French bread, cut in half horizontally (reserve other half for Hot and Crusty Shrimp Sandwich, page 113)
⅓ cup plus ½ cup regular, low-fat, or nonfat mayonnaise
2 teaspoons Dijon mustard
12 ounces thinly sliced cooked turkey
Salt and black pepper
2 medium tomatoes, cored and cut into ¼-inch slices
3 tablespoons finely chopped onion
2 cloves garlic, finely chopped
1 cup grated Parmesan cheese

❋ Preheat the oven to 375 degrees. With your fingers, remove as much bread as possible from inside the half-loaf of bread, leaving a 1-inch-thick crust. Mix ⅓ cup of the mayonnaise and the mustard in a small bowl; spread over the inside and top rim of the bread. Place the bread on a baking sheet and bake for 10 minutes, or until the edges turn brown and the mayonnaise is bubbling. Arrange the turkey slices overlapping inside the bread, making 2 layers. Season with salt and pepper. Top with the tomatoes. Stir together the remaining ½ cup mayonnaise, onion, garlic, and Parmesan cheese. Spread over the top of the sandwich, covering the edges.

❋ Before serving, place on a baking sheet and broil under moderate heat about 6 inches from the heat source until the topping is puffed and golden. Cut into 1½-inch slices and serve immediately.
MAKES SIX SLICES

Leaner: Reduce Parmesan cheese to ½ cup.

One pound cooked turkey yields 3 cups chopped meat.

ORIENTAL TURKEY PASTA SALAD

What do you call a salad that combines Italian pasta, American turkey, and Chinese dressing? Never mind the origin, I call it delicious. The dressing is slightly spicy, but you can cut back on the chili oil, if you prefer it milder.

1 pound spaghetti
2 tablespoons sesame oil
3 to 4 cups cubed cooked turkey
    (¼-inch cubes)
1 bunch green onions with tops, sliced
1 medium cucumber, unpeeled and cut into
    thin strips
½ an 8-ounce can (4 ounces) water chestnuts,
    drained and sliced
⅓ cup chopped fresh cilantro or coriander

Dressing
2 tablespoons sesame oil
2 tablespoons vegetable oil
⅓ cup soy sauce
3 tablespoons rice vinegar
½ teaspoon hot chili oil
3 tablespoons minced fresh ginger
2 tablespoons sugar
⅓ cup dry sherry
1 teaspoon salt

✳ Bring a large pot of water to a boil. Add the spaghetti and cook according to package directions. Pour it into a colander, drain, and rinse with cold water, separating the strands with your hands while rinsing. Drain the spaghetti well, place in a large bowl, and toss with sesame oil.

Thai-Inspired Turkey Salad

Stir in the turkey, green onions, cucumber, water chestnuts, and cilantro.

✳ To make the dressing, whisk together sesame and vegetable oils, soy sauce, vinegar, chili oil, ginger, sugar, sherry, and salt in a small bowl. Pour the dressing over the pasta and toss well. Cover and marinate 1 to 2 hours at room temperature, tossing occasionally.

The salad may be covered and refrigerated overnight. Bring to room temperature before serving.

MAKES 6 MAIN-DISH SERVINGS

TURKEY TOSS

Chop leftover turkey and toss it into omelets, soups, salads, casseroles, tacos, and Chinese stir-fry.

THAI-INSPIRED TURKEY SALAD

Peanut butter, yogurt, cilantro, curry powder, and fruit may sound like an unlikely combination. But, after you taste this salad, I know you'll agree they make a dynamite combination. Don't wait for leftover turkey to make this; it's great with chicken as well.

Dressing
¾ cup regular, low-fat, or nonfat plain yogurt
¼ cup chunky peanut butter
2 tablespoons plus 2 teaspoons lemon juice
1 tablespoon curry powder
¼ cup chopped fresh cilantro or coriander
¼ cup chopped green onions with tops
¼ teaspoon salt
Several dashes of cayenne pepper

Salad
1 large apple, cored and chopped into
    ½-inch pieces
1 orange, peeled and cut into small pieces
4 cups chopped cooked turkey
    (about 1-inch pieces)
2 tablespoons coarsely chopped peanuts

✳ To make the dressing, stir together the yogurt, peanut butter, lemon juice, curry powder, cilantro, green onions, salt, and cayenne in a small bowl.

✳ Place the apple, orange, and turkey in a salad bowl. Add the dressing and toss until well blended.

The salad may be refrigerated for up to 4 hours.

✳ Before serving, toss well and sprinkle with peanuts.

SERVES 4

TURKEY-RICE CASSEROLE

Layers of turkey, rice, zucchini, chilies, and tomatoes are covered with a seasoned sour cream topping to make a simple, colorful meal in a casserole dish.

⅔ cup uncooked white rice
½ teaspoon salt
1 to 2 cups chopped cooked turkey
2 medium zucchini (about ½ pound),
    sliced ¼-inch thick
¾ cup (about 3 ounces) shredded regular
    or low-fat jack cheese
1 can (4 ounces) diced green chilies, drained
2 medium ripe tomatoes

Topping
1 cup regular, low-fat, or nonfat sour cream
½ onion, finely chopped

2 cloves garlic, minced, or 1 teaspoon
    garlic powder
½ teaspoon dried oregano, crumbled
½ teaspoon salt
Black pepper
¾ cup (about 3 ounces) shredded regular
    or low-fat jack cheese

✳ Cook the rice in 1 cup water with ½ teaspoon salt according to package directions. Cool to room temperature.

✳ Preheat the oven to 350 degrees. Grease or spray a 7 x 11-inch (2-quart) glass baking dish. Spread the rice over the bottom. Arrange the turkey over the rice. Place zucchini over the turkey. Sprinkle with the jack cheese. Top with the chilies. Cut off and discard the stem ends of the tomatoes. Cut into thin slices and cut each slice in half. Arrange the tomato slices close to each other over the chilies.

✳ To make the topping, stir the sour cream, onion, garlic or garlic powder, oregano, salt, and pepper in a small bowl. Spread over the tomatoes. Sprinkle with the jack cheese.

The casserole may be covered and refrigerated overnight.

✳ Bake for 30 minutes, or until the mixture is bubbling and the cheese is melted.

To eat is human; to digest, divine.
Charles Townsend Copeland

SERVES 6

A CHRISTMAS RECIPE

Mix a cup of thankfulness

With an ounce of loving care,

Add a dash of hopefulness

And an early morning prayer.

Stir in some generosity

And a smile to light the way

Combine them all

      with peace on earth

For a perfect Christmas day.

Marlene Sorosky

A S W E *finish being thankful for the nation's bounty, Christmas festivities begin. Allow time to bring the spirit of Christmas into your home with earthy-scented greenery, crisp red poinsettias and sparkling ornaments. Place a small bough or garland in each room to help spread holiday cheer and fragrance throughout the house. It's a cozy time of year when one becomes more attuned to detail: baking a gift for someone just because you care, preparing a winter feeder for the woodland crea-*

tures, and writing warm messages on notes and cards. It's that special time when we open our homes and treat our guests to glorious food at Christmas teas, sumptuous buffets, and Yuletide feasts. From holiday cheer to fill your punch bowl, to easy dishes for your youngster's party, to imaginative wreaths to hang on your door, this chapter encompasses a delectable array of foods and creations sure to satisfy your appetites and inundate your senses with Christmas.

ABOUT TEATIME

Afternoon tea began in England. Some say the Prince of Wales began it in the 1870s when Victoria was queen. Finger sandwiches and dainty sweets were traditionally served to tide one over to the late dinner hour. Today teatime offers a respite from our daily routine. Sitting and sipping tea brings a sense of peace and tranquillity to our otherwise hectic lives.

BRIE WALDORF TEA SANDWICHES

Creamy Brie, juicy apples, and crunchy nuts bring contrasting texture and taste to these easy open-face sandwiches.

4 ounces Brie cheese, at room temperature

1 cup finely diced peeled apple
  (about ½ large apple)

¼ cup finely chopped walnuts

1 tablespoon sour cream

7 slices thin-sliced wheat bread

2 small red apples

Lemon juice

❋ In a small bowl, combine the cheese, diced apple, walnuts, and sour cream; mix with a fork. Remove the crusts from the bread and spread with the cheese mixture. Cut into triangles.

The sandwiches may be well covered and refrigerated for up to 6 hours.

❋ Before serving, remove the cores from the apples and cut the unpeeled apples into thin slices. Brush the slices with lemon juice; drain on paper towels, if necessary. Place a slice of apple atop each sandwich.

MAKES 28 SANDWICHES

ORANGE-APRICOT TEA SANDWICHES

This bread stood out among the many that were served at a charity fundraiser. It took several months to track down the recipe, and I don't know whose it is, but it has been well worth the effort to obtain it. Although I'm including it here as part of tea sandwiches, it is tasty enough to stand on its own without a spread. I especially enjoy serving it with a luncheon salad.

Orange-Apricot Bread

½ cup dried apricots

Boiling water

Grated peel of 1 orange

½ cup golden raisins

2 tablespoons butter or margarine,
  at room temperature

1 cup sugar

1 large egg, at room temperature

1 tablespoon vanilla extract

¾ cup boiling water

¼ cup orange juice

2 cups all-purpose flour

2 teaspoons baking powder

½ teaspoon baking soda

¼ teaspoon salt

½ cup chopped pecans

Spread

1 package (8 ounces) whipped cream cheese,
  at room temperature

¼ cup sour cream

❋ Preheat the oven to 350 degrees. Grease and flour a 9 x 5 x 3-inch loaf pan. Place the apricots in a medium bowl and cover them with boiling water; soak for 30 minutes. Drain well. Place the apricots in a food processor fitted with the metal blade. Add the orange peel and raisins; process until pureed. Remove the fruit to a small bowl.

❋ Mix the butter and sugar in the food processor until well blended. Add the egg and vanilla extract, and mix well. Mix in ¾ cup boiling water, orange juice, and pureed apricot mixture, and process until well blended. Add the flour, baking powder, baking soda, and salt; pulse until the batter is thoroughly moistened. Add the nuts and pulse until they are incorporated. Pour the batter into the prepared pan, smoothing the top. Bake for 35 to 40 minutes, or until a cake tester inserted near the center comes out clean. Remove the loaf from the oven and immediately invert onto a cooling rack. Turn right-side up and cool completely.

The bread may be well wrapped and refrigerated for several days, or frozen. Defrost it at room temperature.

❋ To make sandwiches, slice the bread into very thin slices. Stir the cream cheese and sour cream together. Spread half the bread slices with the cheese mixture. Top with the remaining slices of bread. Cut each sandwich into rectangles or triangles.

MAKES ABOUT 36 SANDWICHES

SHRIMP-CUCUMBER TEA SANDWICHES

No tea would be complete without these traditional, fancy favorites.

24 slices appetizer-sized pumpernickel bread
Mayonnaise
1 cucumber, about 1¾ inches in diameter
48 cooked baby shrimp
1 bunch fresh dill

✳ Cut the bread into 2-inch rounds, using a cookie cutter. Spread the slices lightly with mayonnaise. Score the cucumber with the tines of a fork and slice into very thin rounds. Place on the mayonnaise. Top each round with 2 shrimp and small sprigs of dill. Place them on a platter, cover with plastic wrap, and refrigerate until ready to serve, or up to 6 hours.

MAKES 24 SANDWICHES

ABOUT SCONES
English scones are the predecessor of the American biscuit. They can be rolled and cut into any shape or pressed in a pie dish and cut into wedges. Because they are made from a simple baking powder dough, they are best accompanied by a flavorful spread.

BANANA CHOCOLATE CHIP SCONES

I've never been able to resist chocolate-covered bananas, so here I incorporate two of my favorite flavors into biscuits.

3½ cups all-purpose flour
½ cup sugar
2½ teaspoons baking powder
1 teaspoon baking soda
¼ teaspoon salt

12 tablespoons (1½ sticks) cold butter or margarine, cut into 12 pieces
⅔ cup very ripe mashed banana (about 1½ bananas, peeled)
1 cup banana yogurt
¾ cup miniature semisweet chocolate chips
1 egg mixed with 1 teaspoon water, for glaze
Chocolate Cream Cheese (recipe follows)

✳ Preheat the oven to 425 degrees. Place an oven rack in the upper third of the oven. Grease or spray a baking sheet. Mix the flour, sugar, baking powder, baking soda, and salt in a food processor fitted with the metal blade or in a mixing bowl. Process or mix at low speed until combined. Add the butter and blend until the mixture resembles coarse crumbs. Add the banana, yogurt, and chocolate chips. Mix until all the dry ingredients are moistened.

✳ Remove the dough to a floured surface and pat it into a ball; it will be sticky. Roll it with a floured rolling pin into a 9½-inch circle, ¾ inch thick. Using a 2-inch round, square, or heart-shaped biscuit cutter dipped in flour, cut out biscuits. Place them about 1 inch apart on a greased baking sheet. Gather up the scraps of dough and pat them into a ¾-inch disk. Continue cutting and patting out dough until all scraps are used.

✳ Brush the tops with egg glaze; you will not use it all. Bake 7 to 10 minutes, or until the scones are golden brown.

The baked scones may be well wrapped and kept overnight at room temperature, or frozen. Reheat them at 350 degrees for 5 minutes, or until hot.

✳ Serve warm, cut in half, with Chocolate Cream Cheese.

MAKES 24 SCONES

Chocolate Cream Cheese
3 ounces semisweet chocolate, chopped into small pieces
¼ cup whipping cream
1 package (8 ounces) whipped cream cheese

✳ Heat the chocolate and the cream in a small saucepan over very low heat or in a small bowl in the microwave, stirring until the mixture is smooth and the chocolate is melted. Set aside and cool to room temperature. Stir the mixture into the cream cheese in a small bowl.
The cream cheese may be covered and refrigerated for several days.
✳ Serve at room temperature.

It is good to remember that the teakettle, although up to its neck in hot water, continues to sing.
Author unknown

LEMON YOGURT SCONES

These scones have a true biscuit texture and a tart lemon flavor. They are heavenly spread with creamy Lemon Curd.

4 cups all-purpose flour
2 tablespoons baking powder
¼ cup sugar
Dash of salt
¼ pound (1 stick) cold butter or margarine, cut into 8 pieces
4 tablespoons grated lemon peel
2 large eggs, at room temperature
⅔ cup lemon yogurt
½ cup currants
1 egg mixed with 1 teaspoon water, for glaze
Lemon Curd, for serving (optional; recipe follows)

✽ Preheat the oven to 425 degrees. Place an oven rack in the upper third of the oven. Grease or spray a baking sheet with shortening or vegetable cooking spray. Place the flour, baking powder, sugar, salt, and butter in a food processor fitted with the metal blade, or in the bowl of a mixer. Process, or mix at low speed, until the mixture is in coarse crumbs. Add the lemon peel, eggs, yogurt, and currants; mix until thoroughly combined.

✽ Remove the dough to a floured surface and pat it into a ball; it will be sticky. Roll it with a floured rolling pin into a 9-inch circle, about ¼ inch thick. Cut out rounds, squares, or hearts, using a 2-inch cookie cutter dipped in flour. Place the scones about 1 inch apart on a baking sheet. Gather up scraps of dough and pat them into a ¾-inch-thick disk. Continue cutting and patting out dough until all scraps are used. Brush the tops lightly with the egg glaze. Bake for 7 to 9 minutes, or until golden.

The baked scones may be covered and kept at room temperature overnight, or frozen. Reheat them at 350 degrees for 5 minutes, or until hot.

✽ Cut the scones in half and serve warm with Lemon Curd, if desired.

MAKES ABOUT 20 SCONES

Lemon Curd

This thick custard makes a great spread for toast and biscuits as well as a filling for cakes and pastries. It also makes terrific hostess gifts, especially when teamed with lemon scones.

3 large eggs, at room temperature
¾ cup sugar
1 tablespoon grated lemon peel
6 tablespoons freshly squeezed lemon juice
    (about 3 lemons)
6 tablespoons (¾ stick) butter or margarine,
    at room temperature

✽ Whisk the eggs, sugar, lemon peel, and lemon juice in the top of a double boiler until well blended. Place over simmering water and cook, whisking constantly, until the mixture becomes thick and shiny and comes just to a boil. Immediately remove top part from the water. Cool slightly, stir in the butter, and cool to room temperature.

Lemon curd may be covered and refrigerated for up to several months. Stir it well before using.

✽ Serve at room temperature.

MAKES ABOUT 1 CUP

Very good with spiced tea: gossip.

BAKEWELL TARTLETS

I'm sure in Derbyshire, England, where these tartlets originated, they weren't made with frozen puff pastry. But I've found it to be the perfect vehicle to fill with raspberry jam and top with a dome of ground almond batter. I've served these little gems alongside chocolate desserts and they've given chocolate some stiff competition.

½ a 17¼-ounce package (or 1 sheet) frozen
    puff pastry, defrosted in refrigerator
¼ cup seedless raspberry jam
3 tablespoons butter, at room temperature
4 tablespoons sugar
1 large egg, at room temperature
¾ cup very finely ground almonds
¼ teaspoon almond extract

✽ Preheat the oven to 400 degrees. Roll out the pastry on a lightly floured surface to about ⅛-inch thickness. Cut out 24 rounds, using a 2-inch cookie cutter. Press the rounds into 1½-inch miniature muffin cups. Prick the bottoms and sides of the pastry with the tines of a fork. Bake for 5 minutes; the pastry

will puff up. Remove it from the oven, and prick with a fork once more to deflate. Fill each cup with ½ teaspoon jam.

✽ To make the topping, mix the butter and sugar with a fork in a small bowl until blended. Mix in the egg, almonds, and almond extract. Spoon a rounded ½ teaspoon of topping onto the jam, covering it completely. Bake the tartlets for 10 to 12 minutes, or until lightly browned. Remove them from the oven and immediately go around the edges of the tartlets with a small knife and remove them to cooling racks. Serve warm.

The tartlets may be covered and kept at room temperature overnight, or may be frozen. Defrost them at room temperature. Reheat them at 400 degrees for 5 minutes, or until they are heated through.

They are best served warm.

MAKES 24 TARTLETS

A PROPER CUP OF TEA

Place loose tea in a tea ball or infuser, then put tea ball into a china teapot. You will need 1 teaspoon of tea for each cup, plus 1 teaspoon for the pot. Pour boiling water over tea and allow to steep 5 to 7 minutes. Take out the tea ball. Pour tea into thin white china cups.

GLAZED FUDGE SQUARES

Rich, moist, and totally chocolate, these fudgy cakes are blanketed with a sleek, satiny chocolate glaze.

¼ pound plus 4 tablespoons (1½ sticks)
    butter or margarine
3 ounces unsweetened chocolate, chopped
1½ cups sugar
1 teaspoon vanilla extract
3 large eggs, at room temperature

¾ cup all-purpose flour
¼ teaspoon salt

Frosting
2 ounces unsweetened chocolate, chopped
2 tablespoons butter or margarine
1 cup powdered sugar
2 tablespoons milk
1 teaspoon vanilla extract

✳ Preheat the oven to 350 degrees. Line an 8-inch square pan with foil; grease or spray the foil on the bottom and sides. Melt the butter and chocolate in a medium saucepan over low heat, stirring until smooth. Cool for 2 minutes. Stir in the sugar and vanilla extract. Add the eggs, one at a time, whisking until smooth. Stir in the flour and salt. Pour the mixture into the prepared pan; spread evenly. Bake for 25 to 35 minutes, or until the top is crusty and a cake tester inserted near the center comes out clean. Cool to room temperature. Lift the cake from the pan by pulling up on the foil; place it with the foil on a flat surface and peel foil from sides of cake.
The cooled cake may be wrapped and refrigerated for up to 2 days, or frozen. Defrost it in the refrigerator.

✳ To make the frosting, place the chocolate and butter in a medium bowl in the microwave on high (100 percent) for 60 to 90 seconds, or until butter is melted; or melt them in the top of a double boiler over hot water. Stir in powdered sugar, milk, and vanilla until smooth. Spread over the top and sides of the cake.
The frosted cake may be covered and kept at room temperature overnight.

✳ Before serving, peel away the foil from the bottom of the cake. Cut the cake into 36 one-inch squares. Refrigerate until serving time.
MAKES 36 SQUARES

STOCKINGS AS PLACE CARDS
Make individualized stockings with your guests' names on them to hang on the backs of their chairs. Fill each stocking with gadgets depicting the person's hobby. For example, for the person who loves Italian cooking, fill the stocking with pasta, spaghetti servers, and various Italian cooking gadgets. For the baker, fill his/her stocking with baking gadgets such as a pastry wheel or whisk. Non-cooks' stockings might be filled with hobby gadgets such as golf balls and tees, joggers' socks, or artists' brushes and water colors.

TO MAKE A FRESH VEGETABLE WREATH
Choose a wire wreath base about 20 inches in diameter and fill it with sphagnum moss. Insert a wooden floral pick into each vegetable and then stick the other end into the moss. Tie loose vegetables such as asparagus together with wire and cover the wire with straw or raffia. Secure vegetables in place with a hot glue gun or glue.

A PARTY IN THE PLAYROOM
PICKUP DRUMSTICKS
MARSHMALLOW FRUIT SALAD
BROWNIES IN A CONE
CUTOUT COOKIES
POPCORN TREES

PICKUP DRUMSTICKS
A favorite with my own children, these crisp, baked drumsticks were served at many of their parties. I prefer pulling the skin off the meat before coating it, but it's not necessary. Don't limit this recipe to drumsticks; it works well with thighs and breasts, too.

¼ pound (1 stick) butter or margarine
3 cups finely crushed whole-wheat-flake cereal
2 packages (1 ounce each) cheese-garlic salad-dressing mix
16 chicken drumsticks

✳ Place a rack in the center of an oven and preheat the oven to 400 degrees. Line two baking sheets with heavy aluminum foil, and grease or spray the foil.
✳ Melt the butter in a pie pan. Stir the cereal and salad-dressing mix together in another pie pan. Dip the chicken in the butter, rolling to coat all sides. Dip the pieces into the crumbs. Redip if necessary, so the chicken is completely coated. Place on foil-lined baking sheets. Bake, uncovered, for 20 minutes. Turn the chicken and bake another 15 minutes, or until it is crisp and golden. Serve immediately, or cool and serve at room temperature.
The chicken may be covered and refrigerated overnight, or frozen. Defrost it at room temperature. Reheat at 400 degrees for 5 to 10 minutes.
MAKES 16 DRUMSTICKS

MARSHMALLOW FRUIT SALAD

Make this salad the night before, so it becomes firm enough to scoop into balls. Served in a peach half and topped with a cherry, it looks like an ice cream sundae.

2 cans (16 ounces each) fruit cocktail,
    well drained then dried on paper towels
1½ cups miniature marshmallows
½ cup flaked coconut
1 cup sour cream
1 can (16 ounces) pineapple rings, drained
2 cans (16 ounces each) peach halves,
    well drained
5 maraschino cherries, cut in half

❋ Stir the drained fruit cocktail, marshmallows, coconut, and sour cream together in a large bowl. Cover and refrigerate overnight.
❋ To serve, place a pineapple ring on each plate. Top with a peach half, cut-side up. Using an ice-cream scoop, place a scoop of salad in each peach half. Top with half a cherry.
SERVES 8 TO 10

BROWNIES IN A CONE

Moist, fudgy brownies bake in cones. When dipped in chocolate frosting and sprinkles, they look just like ice-cream cones. Kids love to eat them and moms love to serve them, because they can be made ahead and won't melt.

12 flat-bottom ice-cream cones
1 box (21 to 23 ounces) brownie mix
1 cup (6 ounces) semisweet chocolate chips
6 tablespoons (¾ stick) butter or margarine
Candy sprinkles

❋ Preheat the oven to 350 degrees. Place the cones in muffin tins or on a baking sheet. Prepare the brownie mix according to the package directions. Spoon the batter into cones, filling three-quarters full. Bake for 30 to 35 minutes, or until the tops are cracked and have risen above the rims of the cones. A cake tester inserted in the center will not test clean. Remove the cones from the oven and cool to room temperature.
❋ Melt the chocolate chips and butter or margarine in a double boiler over hot water, stirring until smooth. Dip the tops of the brownies into the chocolate. If not well covered, dip again. Stand the cones upright and sprinkle the tops with candy sprinkles. Let them stand at room temperature until the chocolate hardens before serving.
The cones may be loosely covered and kept at room temperature overnight.
MAKES 12 CONES

If Grandma is visiting this Christmas, decorate her room with fresh holly or evergreens and make sure she has a glass of cool water by her bed.

HOW TO MAKE
CUTOUT COOKIES

❋ Make 1 recipe of Butter, Chocolate, or Brown Sugar Cookie Dough (pages 90 and 93), as the recipe directs. Let the dough stand at room temperature until soft enough to roll but still very cold. Roll 1 disk between 2 sheets of waxed paper to ¼-inch thickness; freeze in the paper. Continue with the remaining dough, rolling and freezing. Remove from the freezer, 1 sheet at a time, and cut into desired shapes, using cookie cut-

ters. Reroll and cut scraps until all dough is used. Place them on baking sheets which are either greased or lined with parchment paper.
❋ Preheat the oven to 325 degrees. Bake the cookies for 8 to 12 minutes, or until they begin to brown around the edges and are slightly firm to the touch. Do not overbake, because these cookies firm up as they cool. Cool them slightly on the baking sheets and remove with a spatula to racks while still warm.
Cutout cookies freeze beautifully.

HOW TO DECORATE
CUTOUT COOKIES

❋ Cookies may be decorated either before or after baking. To decorate before baking, sprinkle the cookies with chopped nuts, candied sprinkles, or colored sugar. To decorate after baking, frost them with dark or white chocolate, melted in the microwave or the top of a double boiler over hot water, or with colored frosting. You may either spread the frosting on with a small knife or pipe it through a pastry bag. Supermarkets sell prepared colored frostings in plastic tubes with piping tips already attached. Use a dot of chocolate or frosting to attach candies. To sandwich 2 cookies together, spread chocolate or jam between them

To make a cookie place card, use frosting to write a name on one cookie. Place a dab of frosting in the center of another cookie and use it as a stand to hold the decorated cookie upright. Support it until it dries. (Page 43)

Allow your children to invite their favorite dolls and teddy bears, for they like parties, too. To keep your young guests busy, let them make their own popcorn tree to munch on or take home.

POPCORN TREES
So cute and festive, and best of all, they are entirely edible.

2½ cups powdered sugar, sifted
1 egg white
1½ tablespoons water
6 drops green food coloring
6 sugar cones
3 cups popped corn (½ cup for each cone)
Red cinnamon candies

✸ Stir the powdered sugar, unbeaten egg white, and water together to make a frosting. Tint it with food coloring. Spread the frosting over the outside of the cones, using about 2 tablespoons per cone to cover them completely. While the icing is still soft, press popped corn all over the surface of the cones. Dot with red cinnamon candies.
MAKES 6 TREES

SANTA'S SNACK
Let your children make a sturdy sandwich and a cup of hot mulled cider for a very cold and hungry Santa. He loves anything kids make: peanut butter, peanut butter and grape jelly, peanut butter and ham, peanut butter and cheese, peanut butter and marshmallows. On second thought, maybe you'd better tell them to make two.

A SUMPTUOUS HOLIDAY BUFFET

A Selection of Hot Appetizers

MINI CORN MUFFINS WITH CHILIES AND CHEESE
OVEN-FRIED SESAME EGGPLANT
OVEN-FRIED POTATO SKINS
CRAB-STUFFED MUSHROOMS
ROASTED GARLIC DIP
ZUCCHINI SAUSAGE SQUARES
TAMALE TARTLETTS
CHINESE CHICKEN DRUMETTES
ITALIAN MEATBALLS IN MARINARA SAUCE
PORK SATE WITH PEANUT SAUCE

A Selection of Cold Appetizers

MAPLE-GLAZED ROAST PORK WITH MAPLE-MUSTARD SAUCE
BROCCOLI-CAULIFLOWER TREE
CALCUTTA SMOKED TURKEY SPREAD
SHRIMP WITH VODKA DIP
ROASTED RED BELL PEPPER DIP
ENDIVE LEAVES WITH GORGONZOLA
EGGPLANT SPREAD WITH PITA BREAD

A Selection of Sweets

CHOCOLATE-WRAPPED FUDGE CAKE
SPIRITED EGGNOG CAKE
LUSCIOUS LEMON SQUARES

A SELECTION OF HOT APPETIZERS

MINI CORN MUFFINS WITH CHILIES AND CHEESE

All-American corn bread is baked into tiny muffins, which are scooped out and filled with zesty Cheddar cheese and Mexican chilies. Warm, toasty, colorful, and creative, they are the new appetizer you've been searching for.

Creamed-Corn Muffins
¼ pound (1 stick) butter or margarine
½ cup whole or low-fat milk
1 large egg, at room temperature
1 can (8½ ounces) creamed corn, undrained
1 cup all-purpose flour
1 cup yellow cornmeal
1 tablespoon sugar
1 tablespoon baking powder
1 teaspoon salt
2 or 3 dashes of Tabasco sauce

Filling
1 can (7 ounces) diced green chilies, drained
1 jar (2 ounces) chopped pimientos, drained
1½ cups (about 6 ounces) shredded sharp Cheddar cheese
1 teaspoon chili powder

✸ To make the muffins, preheat the oven to 425 degrees. Grease or spray thirty-six 1½-inch miniature muffin cups. In a large microwave-safe bowl or saucepan, melt butter. Cool slightly, then whisk in milk. Whisk in egg and corn. Stir in the flour, cornmeal, sugar, baking powder, salt, and Tabasco; the batter will be lumpy. Spoon the batter into muffin cups, filling them almost to the top. Bake for 15 to 20 minutes, or until the tops are golden and a cake tester inserted in the

center comes out clean. Immediately remove the muffins from the tins and cool to room temperature.

✳ To make the filling, stir chilies, pimientos, cheese, and chili powder together in a bowl.

✳ Using a small, sharp knife, cut around the tops of the muffins about ¼ inch from their rims. Cut down toward the bottoms of the muffins and remove some of the bread; discard the tops. Spoon the filling into the muffins, mounding the tops.

Filled muffins may be covered and refrigerated overnight, or frozen. Defrost them at room temperature.

✳ Before serving, preheat the oven to 400 degrees. Place the muffins on baking sheets and bake for 5 minutes, or until the cheese is melted.

MAKES 36 MINI MUFFINS

Faster: Stir filling ingredients into the muffin batter and bake as directed. This will make about 55 mini muffins.

OVEN-FRIED SESAME EGGPLANT

Although they taste fried, the crisp sesame crust coating on these eggplant triangles comes from toasting in the oven. One corner of my freezer is always filled with these fabulous hors d'oeuvres, ready for unexpected guests.

¾ cup saltine cracker crumbs (12 double saltine crackers)
½ cup grated Parmesan cheese
¼ cup sesame seeds
¼ teaspoon black pepper
1 medium eggplant (about 1¼ pounds)
Regular, low-fat, or nonfat mayonnaise

✳ Preheat the oven to 400 degrees. Grease or spray 2 baking sheets. Stir the cracker crumbs, Parmesan cheese, sesame seeds, and pepper together in a small bowl. Cut off the stem and cap of the eggplant and peel the eggplant. Cut it into ½-inch-thick slices. Spread both sides of each slice with mayonnaise. Dip each side into the crumb mixture, pressing lightly so it adheres. Cut each slice in quarters, making four triangles. Place them on the prepared baking sheets. Bake for 10 to 12 minutes, or until the undersides are golden. Turn the triangles over and bake 5 to 7 minutes longer, or until they are golden on both sides.

The triangles may be covered and refrigerated overnight, or frozen. Do not defrost them. Reheat frozen at 400 degrees for 4 to 5 minutes, or until hot.

✳ Serve warm or at room temperature.

MAKES ABOUT 40 TRIANGLES

OVEN-FRIED POTATO SKINS

Cut into strips, crisp potato skins make a super scoop for a dip.

8 large baking potatoes
¼ pound (1 stick) butter or margarine, melted
2 cloves garlic, crushed
½ teaspoon salt
¼ teaspoon black pepper
1 recipe Roasted Garlic Dip (see page 58) or other dip as desired

✳ Preheat the oven to 425 degrees. Rinse the potatoes, dry, and pierce with a fork. Place them on a baking sheet. Bake them for 50 to 60 minutes, or until tender. Cool slightly and cut in half crosswise. Cut each half into quarters.

Scrape out almost all the potato pulp, leaving ¼ inch. Reserve the potato pulp for another use.

✳ Combine butter, garlic, salt, and pepper in a small bowl. Dip the skins in butter mixture and arrange them, skin side down, on a baking sheet. Bake for 15 to 20 minutes, or until golden brown.

The skins may be held at room temperature overnight, or frozen. Reheat them at 425 degrees for 7 to 10 minutes, or until hot.

✳ Serve with the dip.

MAKES 64 POTATO SKINS

CRAB-STUFFED MUSHROOMS

When cleaning mushrooms, don't hold them under running water. They are like little sponges and will absorb it. Just wipe them clean with a damp towel. The filling can be made with fresh or canned crab meat. If using canned, be sure to rinse it first.

18 medium-sized mushrooms (about 1 pound)
7 ounces crab meat, cartilage removed
5 green onions with tops, finely chopped
¼ teaspoon dried thyme, crumbled
¼ teaspoon dried oregano, crumbled
¼ teaspoon dried savory, crumbled
Black pepper
¼ cup finely grated Parmesan cheese
⅓ cup regular or low-fat mayonnaise
Grated Parmesan cheese, for topping
Paprika, for topping

✳ Preheat the oven to 350 degrees. Wipe the mushrooms clean with a damp towel. Remove the stems and discard them. Scrape out the gills and any remaining stem with a spoon, making deep cups.

✳ Stir the crab meat, green onions, thyme, oregano, savory, and pepper together in a small bowl. Stir in ¼ cup Parmesan cheese and the mayonnaise, mixing with a fork until combined. Fill the mushroom caps with rounded teaspoonfuls of the filling, and place them in an ungreased shallow baking dish. Bake for 15 minutes.

The mushrooms may be covered and refrigerated overnight. Reheat them at 350 degrees for 7 to 10 minutes, or until hot.

✳ Sprinkle the tops with additional Parmesan cheese and paprika. Place the mushrooms under the broiler for 2 minutes, or until lightly browned.

MAKES 18 MUSHROOMS

ROASTED GARLIC DIP

I never tell my guests what's in this dip until after they've tasted it. The mysterious ingredient is garlic—lots of it—which takes on a nutty flavor when roasted.

2 heads garlic, with the largest cloves
    available (about 2 ounces each head)
2 tablespoons olive oil
1 package (8 ounces) regular or low-fat
    cream cheese, at room temperature
¼ cup regular or low-fat sour cream
½ teaspoon salt
Black pepper
Oven-Fried Potato Skins (see page 57)
    or chips, for dipping

✳ Preheat the oven to 400 degrees. Peel the heavy outside layer from the heads of garlic, separating the heads into cloves. Place the unpeeled cloves in a pie dish. Drizzle with olive oil. Bake for 30 minutes, or until the cloves feel soft when pressed. Remove them from the oven and cool slightly. Peel the warm cloves by

cutting off the stem ends and pushing the pulp up with the fingers. Scrape the pulp into a food processor fitted with the metal blade. Add cream cheese, sour cream, salt, and pepper, and process until pureed, scraping the sides as necessary. Remove the mixture to a bowl. Serve with potato skins or chips.

The dip may be covered and refrigerated for up to 3 days. Bring it to room temperature before serving.

MAKES 1½ CUPS

THE PERFECT PICK-UP
Guests at cocktail parties usually have a glass in one hand. So choose buffet foods that require no utensils and can easily be picked up.

ZUCCHINI SAUSAGE SQUARES

Appetizer squares will always be popular because they are easy to make, easy to serve, and easy to eat. These are exceptionally colorful and tasty, and they freeze beautifully.

1 pound zucchini (about 2 large)
12 ounces bulk pork or turkey sausage
½ cup chopped onion
4 large eggs
½ cup grated Parmesan cheese
18 Ritz crackers, crushed (about ½
    cup crumbs)
1 teaspoon dried basil, crumbled
½ teaspoon dried oregano, crumbled
⅛ teaspoon black pepper
1 clove garlic, finely minced
1 cup (about 4 ounces) shredded sharp
    regular or low-fat Cheddar cheese

✳ Preheat the oven to 325 degrees. Wash the zucchini, trim off the stems, and shred the zucchini; set it aside. Sauté the sausage and onion

in a medium skillet, stirring to break up the sausage, until all pink is gone; drain off all fat.

✳ Whisk the eggs in a large mixing bowl until frothy. Stir in the Parmesan cheese, cracker crumbs, basil, oregano, pepper, garlic, sausage, and zucchini. Spoon the mixture into a greased 7 x 11-inch shallow glass baking dish, spreading the top smooth. Bake for 25 minutes. Sprinkle the top with Cheddar cheese and bake 15 minutes longer. Remove the dish from the oven, cool slightly, and cut into 1½-inch squares.

The squares may be covered and refrigerated overnight, or frozen. Defrost them at room temperature. Reheat on a baking sheet at 350 degrees for 10 minutes, or until heated through.

MAKES 40 SQUARES

Leaner: Substitute 2 whole eggs and 4 whites for the 4 eggs. Reduce Parmesan cheese to ⅓ cup.

TAMALE TARTLETS

The special ingredient that makes these so simple and delicious is a store-bought tamale, found in the refrigerator or freezer section of most markets. The tamale is crumbled and added to seasoned ground beef and golden corn and then heaped into crunchy, buttery toast cups.

Toast Cups
1 loaf (1 pound) sliced egg bread
    (½-inch-thick slices)
¼ pound (1 stick) butter or margarine, melted

Tamale Filling
½ pound lean ground beef
1 refrigerated or frozen tamale (8 ounces)
½ package (1.25-ounce package) taco
    seasoning mix

¼ cup water

½ can (7 to 8 ounces) Mexicorn, drained

1½ cups (about 6 ounces) shredded
   regular or low-fat Cheddar cheese

✳ To make toast cups, preheat the oven to 400 degrees. Flatten the bread slices with a rolling pin. Cut 2 rounds from each slice, using a 2-inch cookie cutter. Brush each round with melted butter, coating both sides. Press the rounds into 1½-inch miniature muffin cups. Bake for 10 minutes, or until golden brown. Remove the tins from the oven and cool the shells until lukewarm, about 15 minutes. Remove shells from the tins and place on baking sheets.

✳ To make the tamale filling, sauté the beef in a large skillet, breaking it up with a fork, until browned; drain off the fat. Break up the tamale with your fingers and add to the beef. Stir in the taco seasoning mix and water. Cook, stirring, until thickened. Stir in the corn. Divide the filling among the baked shells, mounding the tops and pressing lightly to hold the mixture together. Sprinkle the tops with shredded cheese.

The tartlets may be covered and refrigerated overnight, or frozen. Defrost them, covered, at room temperature.

✳ Before serving, bake at 450 degrees for 7 to 10 minutes, or until hot.

MAKES ABOUT 36 TARTLETS

CHINESE CHICKEN DRUMETTES

✳ To make a drumette, discard the tip of a chicken wing, separate the 2 wing bones, then push the meat up to the top of each, making 2 small drumsticks. You can make them yourself, but they are available in the meat section of many supermarkets. Glazed until deep, rich golden brown, they make a fabulous cocktail party tidbit.

2 pounds chicken wing drumettes (about 24)

1 medium clove garlic, peeled

1 piece fresh ginger, about 1 inch in diameter, peeled

½ cup sake (Japanese wine)

½ cup soy sauce

¼ cup packed light brown sugar

¼ teaspoon crushed dried red chili pepper

✳ Place the chicken drumettes in a shallow 2-quart glass baking dish (do not use aluminum). To make the marinade, drop the garlic and ginger into the feed tube of a food processor with the metal blade in place and the motor running. Process until they are finely chopped. Scrape down the sides. Add the sake, soy sauce, brown sugar, and chili pepper. Process until well blended. Pour the marinade over the drumettes. Cover them and refrigerate for 6 hours or overnight, turning occasionally.

✳ Preheat the oven to 350 degrees. Line a shallow broiler pan or roasting pan with heavy foil. Remove the drumettes from the marinade and arrange them in the pan in a single layer, reserving the marinade. Put marinade in a saucepan and bring to a boil; boil for 5 minutes. Reduce heat to a simmer. Bake the drumettes, uncovered, until golden brown and crusty, turning and brushing with the heated marinade every 15 minutes, about 1¼ hours total baking time.

The drumettes may be wrapped and refrigerated overnight, or frozen. Defrost them, wrapped, at room temperature. Reheat them at 400 degrees for 10 minutes, or until hot.

MAKES ABOUT 24 DRUMETTES

ITALIAN MEATBALLS IN MARINARA SAUCE

These are no ordinary meatballs. The robust flavors of hot sausage, Parmesan cheese, and garlic permeate every bite. Don't limit these marvelous meatballs to party appetizers; your family will love them over pasta.

Meatballs

2 slices firm white or egg bread, crusts removed, torn into small pieces

½ cup whole or low-fat milk

2 cloves garlic

6 sprigs fresh parsley (Italian flat parsley, if available)

1 teaspoon grated lemon peel

1 tablespoon olive oil

⅓ cup grated Parmesan cheese

1 large egg, lightly beaten

¾ pound ground beef

½ pound hot Italian sausage, casings removed

1 teaspoon salt

½ teaspoon black pepper

¼ to ½ cup vegetable oil, for frying

Marinara Sauce

2 cloves garlic

½ onion

1 can (28 ounces) whole Italian tomatoes with basil

2 tablespoons olive oil

Salt and black pepper

2 or 3 drops hot chili oil or Tabasco

✳ To make meatballs, soak the bread in the milk in a small bowl for 5 minutes. Squeeze dry and pour off the milk. Chop the garlic and parsley until finely minced in a food processor fitted with the metal blade. Add the lemon peel, olive oil, Parmesan cheese, and egg; pulse until well blended. Add the beef, sausage, soaked bread, salt, and pepper; mix until well combined. Form the mixture into 40 one-inch balls.

✻ Heat ¼ cup oil in a large skillet. Fry the meatballs in batches without crowding over moderately high heat, turning until they are browned on all sides, about 8 to 10 minutes. Add more oil as needed. Remove the meatballs and drain on paper towels.

✻ To make sauce, drop the garlic through the feed tube of a food processor fitted with the metal blade with the motor running. Add the onion and pulse until chopped. Drain the tomatoes, reserving the liquid. Add the tomatoes to the processor; pulse until they are finely chopped. Heat the oil in a medium saucepan. Add the tomato mixture and the reserved tomato liquid. Simmer, uncovered, over moderately low heat until the sauce is reduced and thickened slightly, about 20 to 30 minutes. Season to taste with salt, pepper, and chili oil or Tabasco.

The meatballs and sauce may be placed in separate covered containers and refrigerated for up to 2 days, or frozen. Defrost them at room temperature.

✻ Before serving, place the meatballs and sauce in a saucepan and cook over moderate heat, stirring occasionally, until heated through. Transfer to a chafing dish to keep warm. Serve with toothpicks.

MAKES ABOUT 40 MEATBALLS

TO MAKE A CANDY WREATH
Decorate a wreath with candies, suckers, and ribbons for a Christmas party.

PORK SATE WITH PEANUT SAUCE

Succulent skewered pork, dipped into a Thai soy-peanut sauce, may be the hottest item at your party.

Pork Marinade
½ cup lemon juice
¼ cup soy sauce
4 cloves garlic, crushed
1½ teaspoons sugar
1 teaspoon salt

2 pounds boneless pork, sliced into strips
    ½ inch thick, 1½ inches long, and
    ¾ inch wide
40 six-inch wooden skewers

Peanut Sauce
½ cup (about 2½ ounces) roasted
    salted peanuts
¼ cup soy sauce
¼ cup rice wine vinegar
2 tablespoons creamy peanut butter
    (do not use old-fashioned style)
2 tablespoons fresh lime juice
1 tablespoon seeded minced jalapeño
    chili pepper
1 tablespoon honey
½ teaspoon chili powder

✻ To make the marinade, stir together the lemon juice, soy sauce, garlic, sugar, and salt in a medium bowl or large plastic bag. Add the pork strips, toss well, and marinate, covered, in the refrigerator for at least 4 hours or overnight. Meanwhile, soak the skewers in ice water for at least 1 hour to prevent them from burning; remove from the water and drain.
✻ To make the peanut sauce, grind the peanuts in a food processor with the metal blade. Add soy sauce, vinegar, peanut butter, lime juice, jalapeño, honey, and chili powder. Process until well blended.

The sauce may be refrigerated for up to 3 days.
✻ To assemble, drain pork, discarding marinade. Thread 3 pork strips lengthwise, accordion style, on each skewer. Broil the pork under a very hot broiler for 2 to 3 minutes on each side, or until browned on the outside and pink inside. Or, grill over hot coals.
The pork may be refrigerated overnight, or frozen. Defrost it at room temperature. Reheat it on a baking sheet at 450 degrees for 3 to 4 minutes, or until hot.
✻ Bring the sauce to room temperature and spoon it into a shallow serving bowl. Place the pork on a platter and serve with the sauce for dipping.
MAKES 40 PIECES

A SELECTION OF COLD APPETIZERS

MAPLE-GLAZED ROAST PORK WITH MAPLE-MUSTARD SAUCE

This sweetly glazed pork is a welcome change from the traditional holiday ham. It's great for a buffet because it's presliced, spread with sauce, and then reassembled.

Glaze
½ cup vegetable oil
½ cup finely chopped onion
2 cups maple syrup
½ cup cider vinegar
3 tablespoons Dijon mustard
2½ tablespoons dry mustard
    (Colman's preferred)
1 teaspoon black pepper

1 four-pound boneless loin pork roast
Thinly sliced pumpernickel or rye bread,
    for serving

Maple-Mustard Sauce
1 cup half-and-half
3 tablespoons dry mustard
    (Colman's preferred)
1 tablespoon all-purpose flour
½ cup maple syrup
½ teaspoon salt
2 large egg yolks, at room temperature
¼ cup cider vinegar
2 tablespoons Dijon mustard

✷ To make the glaze, whisk the oil, onion, maple syrup, vinegar, Dijon and dry mustards, and pepper in a medium saucepan. Place the pan over moderately high heat and boil, stirring occasionally, until the mixture is reduced to 1¾ cups, about 20 minutes. Divide in half; refrigerate half for reassembling the cooked roast and use half for basting the roast during cooking.

✷ Preheat the oven to 425 degrees. Dry the pork with paper towels and remove as much fat as possible. Brush the glaze over the entire roast. Place the roast on a rack in a shallow pan lined with foil. Roast for 30 minutes, brushing with the glaze every 15 minutes. Reduce the oven temperature to 375 degrees. Bake for 35 to 45 more minutes, or until a meat thermometer inserted in the middle of the roast reads 150 degrees. Brush the roast with glaze every 10 minutes. Remove the roast from the oven and cool to room temperature. Wrap it in foil and refrigerate until it is well chilled.

✷ To make maple-mustard sauce, mix half-and-half and dry mustard in a medium saucepan. Let the mixture sit 5 minutes to soften the mustard. Whisk in the flour, maple syrup, salt, egg yolks, vinegar, and Dijon mustard. Cook over moderate heat, whisking con-stantly, until the mixture comes to a full boil and thickens. Boil for 1 minute, whisking constantly. Remove it from the heat, place in a bowl and cover with plastic wrap directly on the surface. The sauce may be refrigerated, covered, for several weeks. Stir before using. Serve at room temperature.

✷ Slice the meat as thin as possible; do not be concerned if some of the pieces fall apart. Spread one side of each slice with the reserved refrigerated glaze and press the slices together, reforming the roast. Tie the roast with string to hold it together. Rewrap it in foil and refrigerate for several hours or overnight.

✷ Several hours before serving, bring the roast to room temperature. Remove the string and place the roast on a serving platter. Discard any juices which collect in the foil. Serve the roast at room temperature with desired bread and Maple-Mustard Sauce.

MAKES ABOUT 30 THIN SLICES;

SERVES 14 TO 16 AS PART OF A BUFFET

BROCCOLI-CAULIFLOWER TREE

Let this beautiful vegetable arrangement be the star of your buffet. Served with a vibrant Red Bell Pepper Dip (page 65), it is a natural for holiday parties.

4 pounds broccoli
4 pounds cauliflower (2 medium heads)

✷ Cut the stalks off the broccoli and trim it into serving-size florets. Remove the core from the cauliflowers and cut or break them into serving-size florets. Bring a large pot of salted water to a boil. Cook the cauliflower until crisp-tender, about 5 minutes. Remove it with a slotted spoon and place it in a bowl of ice water to stop the cooking. Add the broccoli to the same water and cook until crisp-tender, 3 to 4 minutes, being careful not to overcook. Place the broccoli in a bowl of ice water. Drain the vegetables well and blot on paper towels.

✷ Choose a 2- to 3-quart deep, conical or round bowl. Beginning in the center, alternate circles of the vegetables, floret-side down, covering the bottom and sides of the bowl. Continue layering rows, fitting the vegetables as close together as possible and making sure the center of the bowl is well packed. Place a plate over the vegetables and weigh down with a brick or tin cans. Refrigerate for at least 6 hours or overnight.

✷ Before serving, remove weights and invert the bowl over the sink, holding the plate and pouring off any excess juices. Invert onto a platter. Serve with Roasted Red Bell Pepper Dip (page 65), if desired.

SERVES 10 TO 12

STORING CUT VEGETABLES FOR CRUDITÉS

To conserve space, store cut vegetables in resealable plastic bags, keeping each vegetable separate. Fill the bags with ice water and then close them securely. Store them in the refrigerator or in an ice chest filled with regular or blue ice.

CALCUTTA SMOKED TURKEY SPREAD

If you are looking for a spread that goes together in minutes and always receives raves, you've just found it. Smoky turkey is high-lighted with curry powder and frosted with chutney.

1 pound smoked turkey, cut into chunks
    (about 4 cups chopped)
2 packages (3 ounces each) regular or
    low-fat cream cheese, at room
    temperature, cut into cubes
4 green onions, cut into chunks
¼ teaspoon Tabasco
2½ teaspoons curry powder
½ to 1 cup chutney (the amount will depend
    on the size of mold)
Crackers, for serving

✳ Spray a 3- to 4-cup bowl, soufflé dish, or
mold with vegetable coating and line with
plastic wrap.
✳ In a food processor with the metal blade,
process turkey, cream cheese, green onions,
Tabasco, and curry powder until well blended.
Spread into prepared dish. Refrigerate for several hours, or until firm.
*The spread may be well covered and refrigerated
for up to 2 days.*
✳ Invert spread onto a platter. Remove plastic wrap. If chutney is chunky, finely chop the
large pieces. Spread chutney over the top and
sides of spread. Serve with crackers.
SERVES 12

SHRIMP WITH VODKA DIP

Although the base of this dip may remind
you of Thousand Island dressing, when it's
enlivened with vodka, it takes on a brand-new
flavor.

2 cups regular, low-fat, or nonfat mayonnaise
¼ cup regular or low-fat sour cream
¾ cup bottled red chili sauce
¼ teaspoon Tabasco
4 teaspoons A-1 sauce
2 tablespoons finely chopped chives or
    green onion tops

Black pepper
⅓ cup vodka
Chilled peeled cooked shrimp, for dipping

✳ Whisk together mayonnaise, sour cream,
chili sauce, Tabasco sauce, A-1 sauce, chives,
pepper, and vodka in a small bowl until combined. Cover the bowl and refrigerate several
hours for the flavors to blend.
*The dip may be covered and refrigerated
overnight.*
✳ Before serving, place the dip in a serving
bowl and surround with shrimp.
MAKES 3½ CUPS

HOW MUCH FOR HOW MANY?
*A rule of thumb for cocktail parties is to allow
ten hors d'oeuvres per person. Begin with a
variety of five for the first twenty guests and add
another selection for every eight additional people. Serve equal choices of hot and cold dishes.*

ROASTED RED BELL PEPPER DIP

Roasted red bell peppers have a naturally
superb flavor, so all you need to do is puree
them to create a delectable dip.

4 large red bell peppers
1 tablespoon vegetable oil
Salt and white pepper

✳ To roast the peppers, preheat the broiler to
its highest setting. Line the broiler rack with
foil and place it so the tops of the peppers are
about 4 inches from the heat. Broil the peppers, turning them on all sides, until their
skins are charred all over. Remove the peppers and wrap them in a kitchen towel or a
paper bag to steam for 10 minutes. Transfer
them to a colander and rinse under cold run-

ning water until cool enough to handle. Peel
the skins off under the running water. Cut out
the cores and seeds and chop the flesh. Puree
the peppers with the oil in a food processor
fitted with the metal blade or in a blender in
batches until smooth. Season to taste with
salt and pepper.
*The dip may be covered and refrigerated for
up to 2 days.*
MAKES 1½ CUPS

ENDIVE LEAVES WITH GORGONZOLA

You may not have thought of filling endive
leaves, but their decorative shape, crisp texture, and ease of preparation make them an
ideal addition to any hors d'oeuvre buffet.

3 heads endive
6 ounces Gorgonzola cheese,
    at room temperature
4 tablespoons mayonnaise
Paprika and/or alfalfa sprouts, for garnish

✳ Cut off the stem ends of the endive.
Separate the leaves, cut off any brown edges,
and place the leaves on a platter. In a food
processor fitted with the metal blade blend
the Gorgonzola and mayonnaise until
creamy; it will be slightly lumpy. Using a knife
or a small spoon, scoop approximately 1 tea-
spoonful of the cheese mixture onto the
widest end of each leaf. Garnish with paprika
and/or alfalfa sprouts. Cover the filled leaves
and refrigerate them until chilled. Serve
chilled or at room temperature.
*The stuffed endive may be covered and refrig-
erated for up to 4 hours.*
MAKES 30 TO 40, DEPENDING ON SIZE OF HEADS

EGGPLANT SPREAD WITH PITA BREAD

This Middle Eastern delicacy, spiced with cayenne and cumin, will wow your taste buds. To turn this spread into an exotic salad, cut the eggplant into larger chunks and spoon it into lettuce leaves.

1 large eggplant (about 1½ pounds)
½ to ¾ cup olive oil
2 cloves garlic, crushed
2 stalks celery, chopped (about 1 cup)
1 green bell pepper, seeded and chopped
1 can (8 ounces) tomato sauce
¼ teaspoon cayenne pepper
1 tablespoon ground cumin
2 tablespoons sugar
2 teaspoons salt
¼ cup red wine vinegar
¼ cup chopped fresh parsley
Pita bread, for serving

❋ Cut the unpeeled eggplant into ¼-inch cubes. Heat ½ cup olive oil in a large skillet. Sauté the eggplant over moderately high heat, stirring, until golden brown, about 10 minutes. Add the garlic, celery, and bell pepper. Cook, stirring, until the vegetables are crisp-tender, adding more oil if needed. Stir in the tomato sauce, cayenne, cumin, sugar, salt, vinegar, and parsley. Simmer, covered, for 10 minutes. Uncover and simmer 10 minutes longer, or until the vegetables are soft. Cool, cover, and refrigerate several hours or overnight.
The dip may be placed in a covered container and refrigerated for up to 1 week, or frozen. Defrost it in the container in the refrigerator.
❋ Before serving, cut the pita bread in wedges and serve with the dip.
MAKES ABOUT 4 CUPS

A SELECTION OF SWEETS

CHOCOLATE-WRAPPED FUDGE CAKE

This exquisitely wrapped gift package will awe your friends. The surprise contents are alternating layers of dark chocolate cake and crème de cacao–flavored butter cream. This is one present where the wrappings are as good as the gift.

Chocolate Cake
⅓ cup plus 1 tablespoon unsweetened cocoa
    powder, preferably Droste Dutch process
2 tablespoons butter or margarine, at
    room temperature
¼ cup boiling water
1 teaspoon vanilla extract
6 large eggs, separated
¾ cup sugar, divided
2 tablespoons all-purpose flour

White Chocolate Buttercream
8 ounces white chocolate, chopped
    (preferably Tobler Narcisse)
¼ cup whipping cream
¼ pound (1 stick) butter, at room temperature
2 egg yolks, at room temperature
    (see Note, page 68)
1 tablespoon light crème de cacao

Decoration
2 recipes White Chocolate Dough
    (recipe follows)
1 recipe Dark Chocolate Dough
    (recipe follows)

❋ Preheat the oven to 350 degrees. Grease a 15½ x 10½ x 1-inch jelly roll pan; line it with parchment or foil, allowing several inches to extend over short ends. Grease or spray the paper (if using foil, flour it also).
❋ To make the cake, place cocoa and butter in a small bowl. Stir in boiling water and vanilla extract. In a large mixing bowl with electric mixer, beat egg yolks with ½ cup of the sugar until very thick and pale, about 4 minutes. On low speed, mix in cocoa mixture. Mix in flour. In small mixing bowl with clean beaters, beat the egg whites until soft mounds form. Slowly add the remaining ¼ cup sugar, beating until stiff and shiny peaks form. Stir a dollop of whites into cocoa mixture to lighten it and then fold in remainder until no streaks of white appear. Pour the batter into the prepared pan, spreading the top evenly. Bake for 20 to 24 minutes, or until the top springs back when pressed with the fingertips and a cake tester inserted in the center comes out clean. Cool to room temperature.
❋ To make white chocolate buttercream, melt the chocolate in the cream in the top of a double boiler over simmering water, stirring until smooth; cool slightly. Cream the butter with an electric mixer until light and creamy. Beat in the egg yolks, one at a time, mixing until light and fluffy. Mix in the chocolate mixture and crème de cacao on low speed. If the buttercream is too thin to spread, refrigerate until it is thick enough, about 30 minutes.
❋ To remove the cake from the pan, go around the sides of the cake with the tip of a sharp knife. Using the paper ends as handles, pull the cake from the pan and invert it on a cutting board. Pull off paper. Trim the edges of the cake. Cut it crosswise into 3 equal pieces. They will be between 4 and 5 inches wide. Place 1 slice on a piece of heavy foil. Spread it with half the buttercream. Top with the second cake layer; spread with the remaining buttercream. Top with the third layer. Refrigerate until firm.
The cake may be wrapped in foil and refrigerated overnight, or frozen.

✳ At least 4 to 8 hours before using, make white and dark chocolate doughs as recipes direct. Roll 1 recipe of White Chocolate Dough between 2 sheets of waxed paper until about ¼ inch thick. Place over half the cake, trimming the edges even with the bottom of the cake. Fold in the corners like wrapping paper. Repeat with the second recipe of white chocolate dough, meeting in the middle and covering the second half of the cake. Roll out the dark chocolate dough between 2 sheets of waxed paper until about ¼ inch thick and cut it into bands about 1 inch wide. Wrap one band around the width of the cake, covering the seam where the pieces of white chocolate meet. Wrap another band around the length of the cake. Top the dark chocolate with thinner bands of white chocolate dough, if desired. Make bows by forming loops of dark and white dough; press gently into the center of the cake. Refrigerate the cake until serving time or overnight, if desired.

✳ To serve, cut into thin slices.

Note: This frosting contains uncooked eggs, which have been known to carry salmonella.

SERVES 12 TO 14

Dark Chocolate Dough

This dough is pliable enough to roll, cut, or bend into any shape imaginable. It's so much fun to play with, I call it adult play dough. Use it to make triangles, bands to put around cakes, roses, and curls.

1 cup (6 ounces) semisweet chocolate chips
¼ cup light corn syrup

✳ Melt the chocolate and corn syrup in the top of a double boiler over simmering water, stirring with a rubber spatula, until the mix-ture is smooth. Pour into a small bowl and cover with plastic wrap directly on the surface. Let the mixture stand in a cool place for 4 to 8 hours, or until it forms a soft, shiny, pliable dough. Do not refrigerate it.

✳ Remove the dough from the bowl and shape it into a flat disk. Roll it as thin as possible between 2 sheets of waxed paper. Remove the top sheet of paper by carefully pulling back on it. If the dough is too sticky to pull off the paper, let it stand until it becomes firm. Turn the dough over and pull off the second sheet of paper. Cut dough into desired shapes, using pinking shears, if desired.

White Chocolate Dough

White chocolate is chemically different from dark chocolate, so the proportions and techniques for making this dough vary slightly from those for the dark chocolate one. To make two batches of dough, it is better to make the recipe twice, rather than to try to double it.

6 ounces white chocolate, chopped (preferably Tobler Narcisse or Lindt Blancor)
3½ tablespoons light corn syrup

✳ Melt white chocolate and corn syrup in the top of a double boiler over hot water, stirring with a rubber spatula until smooth. Remove to a bowl and cover with plastic wrap directly on the surface. Refrigerate until firm. The dough may be refrigerated as long as desired. Remove it from the refrigerator and bring it to room temperature before using. If it is too hard to remove from the bowl, place it in a warm place to melt slightly. Remove it from the bowl, flatten it into a disk, and roll between 2 sheets of waxed paper. Cut it into desired shapes.

SPIRITED EGGNOG CAKE

Can you imagine getting seventy fabulous pieces of cake from one recipe of batter? Drenched with a heady brandy-and-rum glaze, these moist, nutmeg-scented squares don't need garnishing, but a rosette of hard sauce ensures that they are irresistible.

Eggnog Cake
½ pound (2 sticks) butter or margarine, at room temperature
1½ cups sugar, divided
4 large eggs, separated, at room temperature
3 cups all-purpose flour
1 tablespoon baking powder
2 teaspoons ground nutmeg
1 cup eggnog

Glaze
½ cup sugar
¼ pound (1 stick) butter or margarine
¼ cup water
¾ teaspoon ground nutmeg
¼ cup dark rum
¼ cup brandy

Powdered sugar, for garnish

Hard Sauce (optional)
½ pound (2 sticks) butter, cut into small pieces, at room temperature
2½ cups sifted powdered sugar
4 tablespoons brandy or dark rum

✳ Preheat the oven to 325 degrees. Grease a 15½ x 10½ x 1-inch jelly roll pan; line it with waxed paper or parchment and grease the paper. Cream the butter and 1¼ cups of the sugar in a large mixing bowl with an electric mixer until light and fluffy, about 2 minutes. Beat in the egg yolks. Stir together the flour, baking powder, and nutmeg in a medium bowl. Reduce the mixer speed to low and add alternately the flour mixture in fourths and the eggnog in thirds, beginning and ending with flour. The batter will be thick.

✳ In a separate mixing bowl, beat the egg whites until they are thick and soft. Slowly beat in the remaining ¼ cup sugar, mixing until stiff but still moist peaks form. Stir a dollop of the whites into the batter to lighten it, and then fold in the rest until thoroughly incorporated. Pour the batter into the prepared pan, smoothing the top. Bake in the center of the oven for 25 to 35 minutes, or until a cake tester comes out clean and the top springs back when pressed with a fingertip. Remove the cake from the oven and cool in the pan for 10 minutes.

✳ While the cake cools, make the glaze by bringing the sugar, butter, water, and nutmeg to a boil in a small saucepan. Boil 5 minutes, stirring constantly. Remove the glaze from the heat and stir in the rum and brandy. The glaze will be very thin.

✳ After the cake has cooled for 10 minutes, invert it onto a large platter, baking sheet, or sheet of heavy foil. Brush hot glaze over the entire top of the warm cake until all of it is used. Let the cake sit at room temperature, uncovered, for 1 to 2 hours. Then cover with foil and let sit at room temperature overnight. The cake may be refrigerated or frozen, well covered.

✳ Cut the cake into 1½-inch squares, by making 9 cuts lengthwise and 6 cuts crosswise. Sift powdered sugar lightly over the top.

✳ If desired, make hard sauce: Beat the butter in a bowl with an electric mixer on medium speed until it is smooth and creamy. Slowly add the powdered sugar, beating until light and fluffy. Reduce the speed to low and slowly add the brandy or rum while the mixer is running, mixing until smooth. Refrigerate the sauce until it is thick enough to pipe. Fit a pastry bag with a large rosette tip. Pipe one large rosette onto the top of each square.

The cake may be tightly covered and refrigerated for up to 5 days, or frozen. Defrost it, wrapped, in the refrigerator.

MAKES 70 SQUARES

If you're not serving dinner, be sure to serve some hearty hors d'oeuvres like Maple-Glazed Roast Pork or Italian Meatballs in Marinara Sauce. These are substantial enough to be main dishes.

LUSCIOUS LEMON SQUARES

Classic, custard-like lemon pie filling is baked on a buttery cookie crust. Here's a new way of serving an old favorite to a crowd.

Cookie Pastry
½ pound (2 sticks) butter or margarine,
    at room temperature
½ cup sugar
2 large eggs
3 cups all-purpose flour

Lemon Filling
6 large eggs, at room temperature
1½ cups sugar
1½ tablespoons grated lemon peel
    (2 small lemons)
12 tablespoons (1½ sticks) butter, melted
1 cup lemon juice
1 tablespoon all-purpose flour
Powdered sugar, for garnish

✳ To make the pastry, mix the butter and sugar in a food processor fitted with the metal blade or in a mixing bowl until well blended.

Add the eggs and flour and mix until the dough holds together. Shape it into a ball, then flatten it into a disk. Wrap in plastic wrap and refrigerate until cold enough to roll. *The pastry may be wrapped and refrigerated for up to 3 days, or frozen. Bring it to room temperature until soft enough to roll, but still very cold.*

✳ Roll the pastry on a lightly floured surface into a large rectangle. Transfer to a 10½ x 15½ x 1-inch jelly-roll pan. Press into the bottom and up the sides of the pan with your hands. Refrigerate for 30 minutes. Meanwhile, preheat the oven to 400 degrees.

✳ Bake for 20 minutes, or until the sides are very brown and the bottom is beginning to brown. The sides may shrink slightly. Remove the pastry from the oven and cool to room temperature. Reduce the oven temperature to 350 degrees.

✳ To make the filling, whisk the eggs and sugar in a medium bowl until blended. Add the peel and slowly whisk in the melted butter, lemon juice, and flour until incorporated. Pour the mixture into the prepared crust. Bake at 350 degrees for 20 to 25 minutes, or until the top is lightly browned and set. Cool to room temperature. Cut into 35 two-inch squares. Refrigerate until serving time. *The squares may be covered and refrigerated overnight, or frozen. Defrost them in the refrigerator.*

✳ Before serving, sprinkle with powdered sugar.

MAKES 35 SQUARES

SHORT ON REFRIGERATOR SPACE? The refrigerator never seems to hold enough food at party time. Make extra space by storing dips, spreads, cheeses, vegetables, and fruits in an ice chest chilled with regular or blue ice.

*THE NIGHT BEFORE
CHRISTMAS DINNER*
OYSTER CHOWDER
BUTTER LETTUCE SALAD
WITH DRIED CRANBERRIES
AND ORANGES
VEAL STEW WITH FORTY
CLOVES OF GARLIC
HERBED CHEESE POPOVERS
NOODLES WITH BUTTERED
BREAD CRUMBS
CHOCOLATE MOUSSE ICE
CREAM BALL

OYSTER CHOWDER

Oyster stew or chowder is a traditional early American delicacy at Christmastime. This special version combines succulent oysters with corn, cream, potatoes, and other chopped vegetables. Serve it as a first course or main dish.

4 tablespoons (½ stick) butter or margarine

1 large onion, chopped

2 stalks celery, chopped

2 potatoes (about 1¼ pounds), peeled and cut into ½-inch cubes

2 medium carrots, peeled and sliced into ¼-inch slices

¼ cup chopped fresh parsley

3 cups half-and-half

1 can (17 ounces) creamed corn, undrained

½ teaspoon sugar

¼ teaspoon freshly ground black pepper

1 teaspoon salt, or to taste

1 jar (1 pint) oysters with juice

Oyster crackers, for serving

✳ Melt the butter in a large soup pot. Add the onion and celery and cook, stirring occasionally, until soft. Add the potatoes, carrots,

parsley, and 2 cups of the half-and-half. Simmer, uncovered, for 15 minutes, or until the potatoes are tender. Stir in the corn, the remaining 1 cup half-and-half, the sugar, pepper, and salt.

The chowder may be covered and refrigerated overnight at this point, if desired.

✳ Before serving, add the oysters with their juice, and simmer 5 to 8 minutes, or until their edges curl. Serve immediately with crackers.

SERVES 8

BUTTER LETTUCE SALAD WITH DRIED CRANBERRIES AND ORANGES

For this lovely jewel-like Christmas salad, dried cranberries are tossed with crisp butter lettuce, oranges, and a sweet-and-sour poppy-seed dressing.

Orange Poppy-Seed Dressing

6 orange segments

2 teaspoons honey

3 tablespoons raspberry vinegar

¾ cup vegetable oil

1 teaspoon poppy seeds

Salt and freshly ground black pepper

Salad

2 heads butter or Boston lettuce

1 can (11 ounces) mandarin oranges, drained

¾ cup dried cranberries

✳ To make the dressing, puree the oranges in a food processor fitted with the metal blade or in a blender. Mix in the honey and vinegar. With the motor running, slowly pour the oil through the feed tube. Mix in the poppy seeds. Season to taste with salt and pepper.

The dressing may be refrigerated for several days, if desired.

✳ Wash the lettuce and tear it into bite-sized pieces. Wrap and refrigerate until ready to serve.

✳ Before serving, toss the lettuce with the oranges, cranberries, and as much dressing as needed. Divide among salad plates and serve immediately.

SERVES 8

VEAL STEW WITH FORTY CLOVES OF GARLIC

James Beard made Chicken with Forty Cloves of Garlic famous in this country. His idea inspired me to create this stew. When whole cloves of garlic cook, they acquire a very mellow, almost nutlike taste. I don't actually count the number of cloves; any amount will do. But choose the largest ones possible—they add more interest and texture.

1 ounce dried mushrooms

¼ cup vegetable oil

2½ pounds veal stew meat, leg or shoulder, cut into 1½- to 2-inch cubes

1 large onion, chopped

3 cloves garlic, finely minced

1 tablespoon paprika

1 teaspoon salt

¼ to ½ teaspoon freshly ground black pepper

1 tablespoon grated orange peel

1 teaspoon dried thyme leaves, crumbled

1 can (28 ounces) whole tomatoes, drained

1 cup dry white wine

2 whole heads garlic

1 package (10 ounces) frozen peas

✳ Place the mushrooms in a medium bowl and cover them with boiling water. Soak for 30 minutes, drain, and chop them into small pieces.

✳ In a large, heavy saucepan or skillet, heat the oil. Sauté the veal over high heat until brown, turning to brown all sides. This will

need to be done in batches; do not crowd. As each batch is browned, remove it to a bowl. Reduce the heat to low and add the onion and garlic. Cook until the onions are tender but not brown. Stir in the paprika, salt, pepper, orange peel, and thyme. Return the meat to the skillet and add the tomatoes, breaking them up with your fingers. Add the wine and mushrooms. Stir well, cover, and simmer over low heat for 1½ hours, or until the meat is tender, stirring every 10 to 15 minutes.

The stew may be covered and refrigerated for up to 2 days, or frozen. To freeze, cool it and place it in an airtight container. Defrost it at room temperature and reheat in a saucepan over moderately low heat until heated through.

✳ Place the heads of garlic on a chopping board. Smack the garlic heads with the flat side of a knife or cleaver to separate them into cloves. Fill a small saucepan half full of water and bring it to a boil. Add all the garlic cloves and boil them for 10 to 20 minutes, depending on their size, until they are soft enough to pierce with a fork. Drain, cool, and remove the peel by pushing garlic pulp up from the root end.

If desired, the garlic may be prepared one day ahead and covered and refrigerated.

✳ Stir the garlic pulp and peas into the stew, heat until hot, and serve immediately.

SERVES 6 TO 8

Always taste every dish for flavor. Like an artist, you are never finished until the last stroke of the brush
Author unknown

HERBED CHEESE POPOVERS

Boursin-style cheese and herbs melt into the batter, making these popovers very special.

2 large eggs
1 cup all-purpose flour
1 tablespoon dried basil
1 teaspoon dried oregano
1 teaspoon dried thyme
½ teaspoon salt
1 cup whole or low-fat milk
About 2 tablespoons butter, softened, for pans
1 package (4 ounces) herb and spice cheese
    (such as Boursin or Alouette)
Butter, for serving (optional)

✳ Preheat the oven to 425 degrees. In a mixing bowl with an electric mixer or in a blender, mix the eggs, flour, basil, oregano, thyme, salt, and milk until well blended. If made in a mixer, the batter will be slightly lumpy.

The batter may be covered and refrigerated overnight. Stir well before using.

✳ Place about ½ teaspoon of butter in each of ten 2½-inch muffin cups, popover pans, or custard cups. Place the pans in the oven for 1 to 2 minutes, or until the butter is melted. Fill cups one-third full with batter. Drop 1 teaspoon of cheese into each cup and top with the remaining batter, filling the cups about two-thirds full. Bake in the center of the oven for 25 to 30 minutes, or until the popovers are puffed and browned. Serve immediately, with butter, if desired.

MAKES 10 POPOVERS

NOODLES WITH BUTTERED BREAD CRUMBS

To make fresh bread crumbs, remove crusts from the bread and process bread in a food processor fitted with the metal blade. When crumbs are sautéed, they become so crisp and crunchy they make a delectable topping for tender, soft noodles. Commercially dried bread crumbs just aren't the same.

4 tablespoons (½ stick) butter or margarine,
    at room temperature
¼ cup olive oil
¼ cup chopped fresh parsley leaves
1 cup fresh bread crumbs
1 package (12 ounces) medium or wide noodles

✳ Melt the butter or margarine and oil in a small skillet. Add the parsley and bread crumbs and sauté them over moderately high heat until the crumbs are toasted and crusty.

The bread crumbs may be covered and kept at room temperature overnight. Use at room temperature or reheat them for 5 minutes at 350 degrees, if desired.

✳ Cook the noodles as directed on the package. Drain them and place in a serving bowl or on a platter. Pour the crumbs over the top and toss. Serve immediately.

SERVES 8

CHRISTMASES PAST
In very cold weather the turkey must be brought into the kitchen the night before it is roasted for many a Christmas dinner has been spoiled by the turkey having been hung up in a cold larder and becoming thoroughly frozen; Jack Frost has ruined the reputation of many a turkey roaster.
Thomas Love Peacock (1785–1866)

Butter Lettuce Salad, page 70

CHOCOLATE MOUSSE ICE CREAM BALL

Chocolate mousse encases two favorite flavors of ice cream. At Christmas, use vanilla and pink peppermint, but try varying the flavors with the seasons. The mousse never freezes solid, but stays rich and velvety, adding a new dimension to an ice cream mold. It's important to use a deep, round-bottomed, 8-cup bowl—measure it by pouring in 8 cups of water.

10 ounces semisweet chocolate, chopped
5 large eggs, separated, at room temperature
3 tablespoons creme de cacao
2 tablespoons sugar
1½ pints good-quality vanilla ice cream
1½ pints pink peppermint ice cream
Crushed peppermint candies, for
    garnish (optional)
Small candy canes, for garnish (optional)

❋ Line an 8-cup bowl with plastic wrap. Do not be concerned with the wrinkles. Melt the chocolate in the top of a double boiler over simmering water, stirring occasionally, until smooth. Remove the top part from the water. Whisk in the egg yolks and creme de cacao. In a large mixing bowl with an electric mixer on low speed, beat the egg whites until foamy. Increase the speed to high and beat until soft peaks form. Add the sugar, 1 tablespoon at a time, beating until stiff but still moist peaks form. Stir one-third of the whites into the chocolate mixture, then fold the chocolate into the rest of the whites until blended.

❋ Spoon the mousse into the prepared bowl and freeze for about 1 hour, or until the mousse is firm enough to spread over the bottom and sides of the bowl, forming a thin shell. Return the bowl to the freezer until the chocolate is firm. Soften the vanilla ice cream slightly in the refrigerator and spread it over the chocolate mousse. Return the mold to the freezer until firm. Soften the peppermint ice cream slightly in the refrigerator and spread it in the center of the mold; smooth the top. Cover the ice cream with foil and freeze until solid.

The ice cream ball may be frozen for several months, if desired.

❋ Several hours before serving, invert the bowl onto a serving platter. Remove the bowl and the plastic wrap. Smooth the outside of the chocolate with a spatula. If desired, decorate the top by sprinkling it with crushed peppermint candy and decorate the bottom sides with candy canes. Return to the freezer until firm. Remove the mold from the freezer 20 to 30 minutes before serving to soften enough to cut into wedges.

SERVES 12 TO 14

CHRISTMAS COFFEE CAKES

CINNAMON ROLL
CHRISTMAS TREE

CRANBERRY STREUSEL
COFFEE CAKE

BANANA SPLIT MUFFINS

CHOCOLATE-RASPBERRY
MERINGUE COFFEE CAKE

CINNAMON ROLL CHRISTMAS TREE

Tasty pull-apart cinnamon rolls baked into a tree are an additional gift for your family on Christmas morning. This recipe makes 2 trees.

1 cup whole or low-fat milk
1 tablespoon plus ½ cup sugar
2 teaspoons salt
2 packages active dry yeast
4 to 5 cups all-purpose flour
4 tablespoons (½ stick) cold butter,
    cut into 4 pieces
2 large eggs, at room temperature
4 tablespoons (½ stick) butter, melted
2 tablespoons ground cinnamon
1 egg mixed with 1 teaspoon water, for wash
36 glacéed or candied cherry halves

Glaze
1½ cups sifted powdered sugar
2 tablespoons whole milk

❋ Combine the milk, 1 tablespoon of the sugar, and the salt in a small saucepan. Heat to lukewarm, 110 to 115 degrees. Remove from the heat. Sprinkle yeast over the mixture. Let stand until foamy, about 10 minutes.

❋ Meanwhile, in a large food processor fitted with the metal blade or in a mixing bowl, mix 4 cups of the flour with the cold butter until the butter is incorporated. Add the yeast mixture

and eggs and mix until blended. If using the processor, continue processing for 40 seconds; the dough will form a ball and clean the sides of the bowl. If mixing the dough in a bowl, remove it to a lightly floured surface and knead until smooth, about 10 minutes, adding additional flour as needed. Place the dough in a large oiled bowl, turning to coat all sides with oil. Cover with a sheet of buttered waxed paper and a damp towel. Place in a warm, draft-free place to double in bulk, about 1½ hours.

❋ Punch the dough down, turn it out onto a well-floured surface, and knead lightly. Divide the dough in half and cover one half with a towel while you shape the other. Roll it into an 18 x 8-inch rectangle. Brush with 2 tablespoons of the melted butter. Mix the cinnamon and the remaining ½ cup sugar together; sprinkle half over the dough. Starting at a wide side, roll the dough up tightly, like a jelly roll. Turn seam-side down, and cut the roll into sixteen 1-inch slices, leaving a 2-inch end piece for the trunk of the tree. Arrange rolls on a greased baking sheet, flat sides down, in Christmas tree shape: 1 on top, 1 underneath, 2 in the third row, 3 in the fourth row, 4 in the fifth row, 5 in the sixth row, and the 2-inch piece on its side for the trunk. Place the rolls close together and tuck in the ends. Repeat with the remaining dough, melted butter, and cinnamon sugar; place on a second baking sheet. Cover the trees loosely with plastic wrap and let rise in a warm place for 30 minutes.

❋ Preheat the oven to 325 degrees. Brush the rolls with as much egg wash as needed. Place a cherry half in the center of each roll. Bake the trees in the center of the oven, reversing their position after 10 minutes if baking both racks in one oven. Bake 20 minutes, or until lightly browned.

The trees may be covered and kept at room temperature overnight, or frozen. Defrost them, covered, at room temperature. Reheat at 350 degrees for 15 minutes.

❋ To make the glaze, stir enough powdered sugar into the milk to make a thick glaze. Drizzle it over the warm trees. Cool completely and then move them to serving platters, using 2 spatulas.

MAKES 2 TREES, WITH 17 ROLLS EACH

PLACES TO RISE

Yeast loves warmth. Fill a large soup pot with several inches of simmering water. Cover a cookie sheet with a folded towel and place the bowl with the dough on top. Or if your oven has a warm setting, cover the dough with a towel and place it in the center of the oven. If you don't have a warm setting, then a large shallow roasting pan filled with boiling water can go into the oven under the bowl of dough.

CRANBERRY STREUSEL COFFEE CAKE

Orange juice and cranberries turn a simple batter into a comforting Christmas breakfast cake.

2 cups all-purpose flour
1 cup sugar
1½ teaspoons baking powder
½ teaspoon baking soda
½ teaspoon salt
2 tablespoons butter or margarine, melted
¾ cup orange juice
¼ cup boiling water
1 egg, at room temperature, lightly beaten
2 cups fresh cranberries, chopped in a
   food processor or with a knife

Streusel Topping
½ cup packed light brown sugar
2 tablespoons all-purpose flour
2 tablespoons butter or margarine,
   at room temperature
½ cup chopped walnuts or pecans
1 tablespoon grated orange peel

❋ Preheat the oven to 350 degrees. Grease a 9-inch square pan. Stir together the flour, sugar, baking powder, baking soda, and salt in a large bowl. Add the melted butter, orange juice, boiling water, and egg. Stir with a wooden spoon until blended. Fold in the cranberries. Turn into the prepared pan.

❋ To make streusel, mix the brown sugar, flour, butter, nuts, and orange peel with a fork in a medium bowl until crumbly. Sprinkle over the top of the cake. Bake for 45 minutes, or until a cake tester inserted in the center comes out clean.

The cake may be covered and kept at room temperature overnight, or frozen. Reheat at 350 degrees for 10 minutes before serving, if desired.

SERVES 6 TO 8

BANANA SPLIT MUFFINS

These marvelous muffins are a complete surprise. The bottom layer is a sour cream batter, which holds a slice of banana and some nuts; it is topped with a dollop of coconut meringue. The banana softens during baking to permeate the muffin with its fragrant flavor.

4 tablespoons (½ stick) butter or margarine,
   at room temperature
½ cup sugar
1 large egg
½ cup sour cream
½ teaspoon vanilla extract
1 cup all-purpose flour

½ teaspoon baking powder

½ teaspoon baking soda

Dash of salt

2 egg whites, at room temperature

⅔ cup flaked coconut

1 small banana, cut into ½-inch-thick slices

2 tablespoons chopped walnuts or pecans

6 glacéed or candied cherries, cut in half

✳ Preheat the oven to 375 degrees. In a food processor fitted with the metal blade, or in a mixing bowl with an electric mixer, cream the butter and ¼ cup of the sugar until well blended. Beat in the egg until combined; the batter will be lumpy. Add the sour cream and vanilla extract and mix until well blended. Mix in the flour, baking powder, baking soda, and salt until incorporated; do not overmix.

✳ Grease 12 two-inch muffin cups. Beat the egg whites in a large mixing bowl until soft peaks form. Beat in the remaining ¼ cup sugar, 1 tablespoon at a time, mixing until stiff peaks form. Fold in the coconut.

✳ Spoon 1 heaping tablespoon of the batter into each cup. Top each with a slice of banana and ½ teaspoon chopped nuts. Press in lightly with your fingers. Top each with a heaping tablespoon of coconut meringue. Place a cherry half in the center. Bake for 20 to 25 minutes, or until golden. Cool 10 minutes, then remove from the tins. Serve warm. *The muffins may be well wrapped and kept at room temperature overnight or may be frozen. Defrost them, wrapped, at room temperature. Reheat at 350 degrees for 8 to 10 minutes, or until warm.*

MAKES 12 MUFFINS

CHOCOLATE-RASPBERRY MERINGUE COFFEE CAKE

This is the ultimate coffee cake: a buttery, rich yeast batter is swirled with billowy meringue, raspberry jam, and chocolate chips. The dough doesn't have to be kneaded, but it must be refrigerated for at least 24 hours before you assemble the cake, so be sure to plan accordingly.

Dough

½ pound (2 sticks) butter or margarine

¼ cup whole or low-fat milk

¼ cup sour cream

2⅓ cups all-purpose flour

2 tablespoons sugar

4 packages active dry yeast

3 egg yolks, at room temperature, lightly beaten

Filling

3 egg whites, at room temperature

1 cup sugar

¾ cup seedless raspberry preserves

2 tablespoons ground cinnamon

1 cup (6 ounces) semisweet chocolate chips

½ cup chopped walnuts

1 cup raisins

½ cup flaked coconut

Streusel Topping

4 tablespoons (½ stick) butter or margarine, at room temperature

½ cup sugar

½ cup all-purpose flour

½ cup chopped walnuts

✳ To make the dough, melt the butter with the milk and sour cream in a small saucepan. Cool to 115 to 120 degrees; it should feel very warm on the inside of your wrist. Stir the flour and sugar together in a large bowl. Sprinkle in the yeast. Make a well in the center and stir in

the egg yolks. Stir in the butter mixture with a wooden spoon until well blended. Place a piece of plastic wrap directly on the surface of the dough and cover the bowl with a damp towel. Refrigerate the dough for a minimum of 24 or up to 48 hours.

✳ Remove the dough from the refrigerator and leave at room temperature until soft enough to roll, but still very cold. Meanwhile, make the filling by beating the egg whites in a mixing bowl with an electric mixer until soft peaks form. Gradually beat in the sugar, 2 tablespoons at a time, until the whites are stiff, smooth, and shiny, like marshmallow creme.

✳ Divide the dough in half and roll one half on a lightly floured surface into a 12 x 18-inch rectangle. Spread half the meringue over the dough, leaving a 1-inch border. Spread half the preserves over the meringue. Sprinkle with half the cinnamon, chocolate chips, walnuts, raisins, and coconut. Roll up jelly-roll fashion. Do not be concerned if the dough tears. Repeat with the other half of the dough, filling with the other half of the meringue, preserves, cinnamon, chocolate chips, walnuts, raisins, and coconut.

✳ Grease and flour a 12-cup angel food cake pan. Place one roll around the bottom of the pan. Top with the second roll, placing the ends of the rolls facing each other. Cover with buttered waxed paper and a damp towel and let rise in a warm, draft-free place for 2 to 3 hours, or until doubled in bulk.

✳ Meanwhile, make the streusel: Combine the butter, sugar, flour, and walnuts in a food processor fitted with the metal blade or mix in a bowl with a pastry blender until crumbly. Sprinkle over the top of the cake. Cover and

let rise for an additional hour, or until doubled in bulk.

✳ Preheat the oven to 350 degrees. Bake for 40 to 50 minutes, or until the top is lightly browned and cracked. The cake should have risen to the top of the pan. Remove the pan to a rack and cool the cake to room temperature. Go around the sides with a knife and lift the cake from the pan.

The cake may be covered and kept at room temperature overnight, or wrapped in foil and frozen. Defrost it, covered, at room temperature overnight.

✳ Serve at room temperature.

SERVES 12

The extra warmth in your kitchen during the holidays makes it a cozy place for bread to rise. And when the bread bakes, it exudes such an enticing aroma it will draw everyone to your oven.

DECKING THE HALL

Decorate everything for this festive occasion. From platters garnished with Christmas greens, radish roses, cherry tomatoes, and red and green bell pepper cutouts to tabletops graced with flickering candles, inundate your guests with lavish sensations.

A FESTIVE YULETIDE FEAST

FRESH MUSHROOM AND GREEN ONION SOUP

ROAST BREAST OF TURKEY WITH CRANBERRY-GREEN PEPPERCORN SAUCE

OR PERFECT PRIME RIB ROAST

YORKSHIRE PUDDING WITH WILD RICE

CAULIFLOWER WITH PUREE OF PEAS AND WATERCRESS

SAUTÉED CHERRY TOMATOES

STEAMED GINGERBREAD PUDDING WITH CREAMY VANILLA SAUCE

FRESH MUSHROOM AND GREEN ONION SOUP

When I really want to impress my guests, I serve this elegant soup. It tastes rich and creamy although it contains no cream. The mushrooms impart a fresh, sophisticated taste.

3 large or 4 small bunches green onions
¾ pound mushrooms, cleaned and trimmed
¼ pound (1 stick) butter
½ teaspoon salt, or to taste
½ teaspoon white pepper, or to taste
⅛ teaspoon cayenne pepper
3 tablespoons all-purpose flour
6 cups chicken broth

Garnish
¼ pound mushrooms, thinly sliced
½ cup sour cream
1 large green onion, thinly sliced, for garnish

✳ Coarsely chop the green onions, including the tops, by hand or in a food processor fitted with the metal blade; set aside. Chop the mushrooms; set aside.

✳ Melt the butter in a medium soup pot until foaming. Add the green onions, salt, and white and cayenne peppers. Reduce the heat to low, cover, and cook for 10 minutes, stirring occasionally. Do not brown. Remove the pan from the heat, and stir in the flour. Stir over low heat for 2 minutes. Add the chicken broth and whisk over moderately high heat until the soup comes to a boil. Reduce the heat to moderately low and simmer, uncovered, for 10 minutes, stirring occasionally. Add the chopped mushrooms and heat 1 minute. Puree the soup in batches in a blender or food processor fitted with the metal blade.

The soup may be covered and refrigerated overnight, or frozen.

✳ Before serving, reheat the soup until hot. Taste and adjust the seasonings. Stir sliced mushrooms into the soup. Cook until they are soft, about 1 minute. Ladle the soup into bowls, garnishing each with a dollop of sour cream and a sprinkling of green onion.

SERVES 8

ROAST BREAST OF TURKEY WITH CRANBERRY-GREEN PEPPERCORN SAUCE

If your market doesn't have a boned, rolled turkey breast, ask the butcher to prepare one for you. You may expect a roasted turkey breast to be dry, but when cooked to only 135 degrees on a meat thermometer, it will be moist and juicy and still cooked through. If your roast is smaller than 6 pounds, start checking it at 1 hour. The cranberry-tinged sauce, spiced with green peppercorns, is the perfect complement for this subtly flavored bird.

3 tablespoons vegetable oil

½ teaspoon salt

¼ teaspoon black pepper

½ teaspoon paprika

½ teaspoon poultry seasoning

1 turkey breast (6 pounds net weight),
   boned, rolled, and tied

6 slices bacon

Cranberry–Green Peppercorn Sauce

3 tablespoons drippings from cooked turkey
   or vegetable oil or butter

3 tablespoons all-purpose flour

1 cup Giblet Stock (page 24) or chicken broth

¼ cup dry Madeira wine

1 tablespoon green peppercorns, drained
   if in brine and crushed

¼ cup whole-berry cranberry sauce

❋ Preheat the oven to 400 degrees. Mix the oil, salt, pepper, paprika, and poultry seasoning in a small bowl. Rub all over the turkey. Place the roast on a rack in a shallow roasting pan. Cover the top with bacon. Roast at 400 degrees for 1½ to 1¾ hours, or until a meat thermometer reaches 175 degrees. Baste with the pan drippings every 15 minutes. When the turkey is done, remove the bacon and discard. Place the roast on a carving board. Let rest for 20 minutes while preparing the sauce.

❋ To make the sauce, pour 3 tablespoons of the drippings into a small saucepan. Heat over moderate heat and stir in the flour. Cook, stirring, for 1 minute. Add giblet stock or chicken broth and whisk constantly until the mixture comes to a boil and thickens. Reduce the heat to low and stir in the Madeira, peppercorns, and cranberry sauce. If desired, skim the fat from the pan juices and add the juices to the sauce. Keep warm until ready to serve.

❋ Remove the strings from the roast and slice into thin slices. Spoon some sauce over each slice and pass the remainder.

SERVES 10 TO 12

PERFECT PRIME RIB ROAST

Irene Angelo, owner of Angelo's Market and Cooking School in Modesto, California, shared this recipe with me many years ago. It is so fabulous that I never make prime rib any other way. The technique is a simple formula: When you buy a rib roast, calculate that one rib will serve 2 persons, so for six, you will need a 3-rib roast, without the short ribs.

❋ The timetable for roasting by this method is approximately 15 minutes per rib, or 5 minutes per pound of trimmed, ready-to-cook meat. For example, a 3-rib roast, weighing 8 to 9 pounds, will roast for 40 to 45 minutes.

❋ Bring the roast to room temperature. Preheat the oven to 500 degrees. Place the roast in a shallow roasting pan. Sprinkle with a little flour and rub the flour lightly into the fat; this will help seal in the juices. Season generously with salt and coarsely cracked black pepper. To protect your oven from spattering fat, place a tent of aluminum foil loosely over the top of the meat. Roast according to the above timetable, following the timing exactly. If you have a timer, set it to remind you.

❋ When the cooking time ends, turn off the oven heat, but do not open the door. Allow the roast to remain in the oven for at least 1 hour, or until the oven is lukewarm, about 2 hours.

❋ The roast will be beautifully rare inside and, for as long as 4 hours, retain a crunchy outside and an internal heat suitable for serving.

STEAMED PUDDINGS

Although traditionally cooked on top of the stove, steamed puddings may be more easily cooked in the oven—the temperature is more constant and the water does not boil away.

YORKSHIRE PUDDING WITH WILD RICE

The wonderful crunch and nutty taste of wild rice adds a new dimension to an old favorite.

⅔ cup uncooked wild rice

2 cups water

1 teaspoon salt

4 large eggs

2 cups whole or low-fat milk

1½ cups all-purpose flour

6 tablespoons (¾ stick) butter or margarine

1 beef bouillon cube

1 teaspoon Worcestershire sauce

❋ Place the rice, water, and ½ teaspoon of the salt in a small saucepan and bring to a boil over high heat. Reduce the heat to low, cover, and simmer until the rice is tender, about 45 minutes. Drain off any remaining water. Cool to room temperature.

The rice may be covered and refrigerated overnight at this point.

❋ While the rice is cooking, beat the eggs until frothy in a large mixing bowl with an electric mixer. Beat in the milk, flour, and the remaining ½ teaspoon salt. The batter will be slightly lumpy.

The batter may be covered and refrigerated overnight at this point.

❋ Preheat the oven to 425 degrees. Stir the cooked rice into the batter. Place the butter or margarine in a 9 x 13-inch glass casserole dish and place the dish in the oven until the butter is melted. Remove from the oven and stir in the bouillon cube and Worcestershire

sauce until dissolved. Return the dish to the oven and leave until the butter is sizzling. Pour the rice batter into the dish. Bake in the center of the oven for 20 to 25 minutes, or until puffed and golden. Serve immediately, cut into squares.

SERVES 8 TO 10

CAULIFLOWER WITH PUREE OF PEAS AND WATERCRESS

Snowy white cauliflower, capped with a bright green vegetable sauce, makes a decorative and delicious side dish. Encircled with a wreath of herbed cherry tomatoes, it is a Christmas showpiece.

2 packages (10 ounces each) frozen tiny peas
1½ cups loosely packed watercress leaves
1 cup chicken broth
Salt and black pepper
2 heads cauliflower (1½ to 2 pounds each)
1 recipe Sautéed Cherry Tomatoes
    (next recipe; optional)

✳ To make a puree of peas and watercress, place the peas, watercress, and chicken broth in a medium saucepan. Bring to a boil and cook, uncovered, 3 to 4 minutes, or until tender. Cool slightly and transfer the mixture to a food processor fitted with the metal blade. Process until pureed. Season with salt and pepper to taste.
The puree may be covered and refrigerated overnight. Reheat in the saucepan until hot, if desired.
✳ To prepare cauliflower, trim off the outer leaves and stems. Hollow out the cores with a sharp knife. The heads can be cooked together if you have a deep roasting pan; if not, cook each one separately in a very large pot. Place a rack or steamer basket in the pan and add ¾ to 1 inch of water. Bring to a boil.

Place the cauliflower on the rack, top side up. Cover and steam gently until tender when pierced with a small knife, about 15 to 20 minutes, depending on the size. Drain very well. Sprinkle with salt and pepper, if desired.
✳ To serve, spoon a bed of puree on a large platter, leaving a 2-inch border.
✳ Place the cauliflower on the puree and pull the florets apart with 2 forks to open the heads slightly. Drizzle the remaining puree over the top. Surround with Sautéed Cherry Tomatoes, if desired.

SERVES 8 TO 12, DEPENDING ON SIZE OF CAULIFLOWER

Feasts must be solemn and rare, or else they cease to be feasts.
Aldous Huxley

SAUTÉED CHERRY TOMATOES

Bring the tomatoes to room temperature before sautéing, so they will cook through quickly without bursting.

3 tablespoons vegetable oil
2 tablespoons finely chopped fresh parsley
½ teaspoon dried basil, crumbled
⅛ teaspoon salt
2 boxes (1 pint each) cherry tomatoes,
    at room temperature
1 teaspoon lemon juice

✳ Heat the oil in a medium skillet over moderate heat. Stir in the parsley, basil, and salt, and sauté, stirring, for 2 minutes. Add the cherry tomatoes and cook gently for 3 to 4 minutes, or until heated through. Stir in the lemon juice and serve immediately.

SERVES 10 TO 12

To make good soup the pot must only simmer or "smile."
French proverb

STEAMED GINGERBREAD PUDDING WITH CREAMY VANILLA SAUCE

Bursting with the holiday flavors of gingerbread, this molasses-colored pudding is studded with bright red cranberries. The cool, sweet vanilla sauce superbly complements this festive dessert.

1 orange
2 teaspoons baking soda
½ cup light molasses
⅓ cup sugar
1 large egg, at room temperature
½ teaspoon ground allspice
1½ teaspoons powdered ginger
1½ cups all-purpose flour
2 cups cranberries
Creamy Vanilla Sauce (recipe follows)

✳ Preheat the oven to 350 degrees. Spray a 4- to 6-cup steamed-pudding mold with vegetable coating spray. Grate the peel from the orange and set peel aside. Squeeze the juice from the orange; measure ⅓ cup, and heat until hot. Place the baking soda in a large bowl; stir in hot orange juice until the soda is dissolved. Stir in the molasses, sugar, egg, allspice, ginger, flour, and orange peel. Fold in the cranberries. Spoon the batter into the mold. Cover the top with waxed paper and a lid or foil. Place in a stock pot on a rack, or in a steamer. Pour in enough hot water to come one-third up the sides of the mold. Cover and bake for 2¼ to 2½ hours, or until a knife inserted in the center comes out clean. Remove the mold to a rack and cool for 10 minutes. Invert it onto a platter or foil.
The pudding may be wrapped in foil and refrigerated for several days, or frozen. Defrost

Steamed Gingerbread Pudding

*it, covered, at room temperature. Reheat at
350 degrees for 20 minutes, or until hot.*
❋ Serve warm with Creamy Vanilla Sauce.

SERVES 6 TO 8

Creamy Vanilla Sauce
This thick, sweet whipped-cream topping
does wonders for plain cakes and puddings.

1 cup powdered sugar
3 tablespoons butter or margarine,
    melted and cooled
¼ teaspoon vanilla extract
Dash of salt
1 cup whipping cream

❋ Whisk together the powdered sugar, melted
butter, vanilla extract, and salt in a medium
bowl until well blended and fluffy. Whip the
cream in a separate bowl until soft peaks form.
Fold the whipped cream into the sugar mixture. Serve chilled.
*The sauce may be covered and refrigerated
overnight.*

MAKES 1¾ CUPS

CHRISTMAS CHEER
CRANBERRY DAIQUIRIS
BLOODY MARY PUNCH
RUM PUNCH
CITRUS SPICED TEA
CHILDREN'S PARTY PUNCH
AMBER CHAMPAGNE
SPARKLE
ICE MOLD

CRANBERRY DAIQUIRIS
Colorful daiquiris with a holiday theme.

1 cup crushed ice
1 can (6 ounces) frozen daiquiri mix
¾ cup (6 ounces) rum
½ cup jellied cranberry sauce
1 tablespoon grenadine syrup (optional)

❋ Place the ice in a blender. Add the daiquiri
mix, rum, cranberry sauce, and grenadine
syrup. Mix until the ice is pureed and the
drink is frothy.

MAKES FOUR 5-OUNCE SERVINGS

BLOODY MARY PUNCH
An eye-opening, spicy brunch punch.

2 cans (46 ounces each) spicy tomato juice,
    such as Snap-E-Tom, chilled
2 cans (10½ ounces each) condensed beef
    broth, chilled
5 cups vodka, chilled
⅔ cup fresh lemon juice
2½ teaspoons Worcestershire sauce
½ teaspoon Tabasco sauce
Ice

❋ Stir tomato juice, beef broth, vodka, lemon
juice, Worcestershire sauce, and Tabasco
sauce together in a punch bowl. Add ice.

MAKES TWENTY-SIX 6-OUNCE SERVINGS

RUM PUNCH
This generously spiked punch tastes so good
it sneaks up on you.

1 bottle (750 milliliters) light rum
1 can (46 ounces) pineapple juice, chilled
½ can (6 ounces) frozen orange juice concen-
    trate, defrosted and undiluted
1 quart (4 cups) grapefruit juice, chilled
1 cup (8 ounces) grenadine syrup
1½ cups (12 ounces) apricot brandy
Ice mold (page 88) or ice chunk

❋ Mix rum, pineapple juice, orange juice
concentrate, grapefruit juice, grenadine
syrup, and brandy in a large punch bowl.
Add the ice mold or chunk.

MAKES TWENTY 6-OUNCE SERVINGS

CITRUS SPICED TEA
Citrus juices and spices, teamed with fragrant
black tea, produce a never-fail hot beverage
for a crowd.

1 tablespoon whole cloves
3 cinnamon sticks
12 cups water
15 black tea teabags
1½ cups orange juice
½ cup lemon juice
1 cup sugar

✳ Bring the cloves, cinnamon, and water to a boil in a medium saucepan. Add the tea bags, remove from the heat, and steep 5 minutes; strain. In a separate saucepan, bring the orange juice, lemon juice, and sugar to a boil, stirring until the sugar is dissolved. Add to the hot tea. Serve at once.

MAKES TWELVE 8-OUNCE SERVINGS

CHILDREN'S PARTY PUNCH
For kids of all ages.

2 cans (46 ounces each) pineapple juice, chilled
1 bottle (16 ounces) cranberry juice, chilled
2 bottles (33.8 ounces each) 7-Up, chilled
1 quart rainbow sherbet

✳ Blend the pineapple and cranberry juices in a punch bowl. Pour in 7-Up. Top with spoonfuls of sherbet.

MAKES TWENTY-FIVE 8-OUNCE SERVINGS

AMBER CHAMPAGNE SPARKLE

It is not necessary to purchase the best champagne when mixing it with other liquors. It's the combination of ingredients that makes this punch so special.

1 bottle (750 milliliters) sauternes, chilled
¼ cup (2 ounces) brandy
2 tablespoons (1 ounce) orange liqueur such as Curaçao or Triple Sec
1 bottle (750 milliliters) champagne, chilled
Ice mold (this page) or ice chunk

✳ Mix the sauternes, brandy, and orange liqueur in a punch bowl. Just before serving, add the champagne and the ice mold or chunk.

MAKES TEN 6-OUNCE SERVINGS

ICE MOLD
This recipe is written for a 6-cup ring mold. Follow the directions, increasing the water, and you can use any size mold that will fit in your punch bowl. If you do not wish to dilute your punch too much, use half water and half pineapple or other juice in your ice mold.

6 cups water
Edible leaves such as mint, camellia, or lemon
Fruit such as pineapple rings, lemon slices, orange slices, cherries

✳ Fill a 6-cup ring mold half full of water. Freeze until solid. Remove from the freezer; arrange the leaves and/or fruit decoratively on top of the ice. Carefully pour a small amount of water around the fruit and leaves to hold them in place. Return the mold to the freezer until solid. Add more water to fill the mold to the top, if necessary. Freeze overnight or up to one week. Unmold by dipping the bottom of the mold in cold water; turn out onto heavy foil. If not using immediately, wrap the mold securely in foil and freeze until ready to use. Float in a punch bowl, decorative-side up.

Store several ice molds in your freezer so that when one disappears into the punch you can replace it with another.

THROUGH THE MAIL
Choose sturdy cookies such as Fudge Crackles, Old-Fashioned Date Bars, Chocolate Chip–Hazelnut Squares, White Chocolate Haystacks, and Brownies for sending to distant places. To keep them airtight, place them in a plastic bag, gather the top, insert a straw and suck out the air. Secure quickly. Place in a tin or box and fill empty spaces with unsalted popped corn.

Rum Punch, page 87, with Ice Mold

COOKIES

WHITE CHOCOLATE CHUNK COOKIES

Although white chocolate chips work fine in these rich, buttery cookies, I prefer chopping white chocolate almond bark or a good-quality imported white chocolate into chunks.

9 ounces white chocolate
¼ pound (1 stick) unsalted butter or
    margarine, at room temperature
½ cup packed dark brown sugar
¼ cup granulated sugar
1 large egg, at room temperature
1½ teaspoons vanilla extract
1¼ cups all-purpose flour
½ teaspoon baking soda
Dash of salt

✳ Preheat the oven to 350 degrees. Place a rack in the upper third of the oven. With a sharp knife or food processor with the metal blade, chop white chocolate into coarse pieces. Do not chop fine.

✳ Place the butter and the brown and granulated sugars in a food processor fitted with the metal blade or in a mixing bowl and mix until well blended. Add the egg and vanilla extract and mix well. Mix in the flour, baking soda, and salt, mixing until the flour is incorporated. Mix in the white chocolate. If the food processor is too full and will not mix in the chocolate, remove to a bowl and mix in by hand.

✳ Drop the batter by heaping tablespoons onto ungreased heavy-duty or cushioned baking sheets, placing them about 1½ inches apart. Bake for 10 to 12 minutes, or until the tops just begin to brown. The cookies will appear underdone and doughy; take them out anyway. They will firm up as they cool.

Let them sit for 2 minutes and then remove them with a spatula to cooling racks.

The cookies are best served the same day, or frozen. Defrost them for 10 minutes at room temperature.

MAKES ABOUT 36 COOKIES

OLD-FASHIONED DATE BARS

My grandma's version of this classic cookie has moist cooked dates sandwiched between two crunchy oatmeal pastry layers.

1½ cups (8 ounces) whole pitted dates
1½ cups orange juice
2½ cups all-purpose flour
½ teaspoon salt
1½ cups packed light brown sugar
¾ pound (3 sticks) cold unsalted butter or
    margarine, cut into small pieces
1 cup flaked coconut
1 cup chopped walnuts
1½ cups quick-cooking rolled oats (not instant)
Powdered sugar, for sprinkling

✳ Place the dates and orange juice in a medium saucepan. Simmer over moderate heat, stirring occasionally to break up the dates, for 20 to 25 minutes, or until the mixture is thickened. Remove from the heat.

✳ Preheat the oven to 350 degrees. Combine the flour, salt, brown sugar, and butter in a food processor fitted with the metal blade, or in a mixing bowl with a fork. Mix until the mixture resembles coarse crumbs. Add the coconut, walnuts, and oats, and pulse on and off or stir just until blended.

✳ Press half the pastry into the bottom of an ungreased 9 x 13-inch baking pan. Cover with a sheet of waxed paper. Pat flat. Discard waxed paper. Spread the date mixture over the dough to within ½ inch of the edges. Top with the remaining dough, spreading it evenly and

flattening it slightly. Bake for 35 to 40 minutes, or until golden brown. Remove to cooling racks and cool completely. Cut into 1½-inch squares and sprinkle with powdered sugar.

The cookies may be tightly covered and kept at room temperature for up to several days, or frozen.

MAKES 48

CHOCOLATE COOKIE DOUGH FOR CUTOUT COOKIES

A firm dough, very simple to make and easy to work with.

½ pound plus 4 tablespoons (2½ sticks)
    butter or margarine, at room temperature
1¾ cups powdered sugar, sifted
1 large egg, at room temperature
2½ cups all-purpose flour
½ cup unsweetened cocoa powder
¼ teaspoon salt

✳ Cream the butter and powdered sugar in a mixing bowl with an electric mixer until light and fluffy, about 2 minutes. Mix in the egg and beat for another minute. Add the flour, cocoa, and salt; mix until incorporated. Divide the dough into 3 parts. Flatten each into a disk and wrap in plastic wrap. Refrigerate until firm. Use as directed for Cutout Cookies (page 52).

The dough may be wrapped in plastic wrap and refrigerated for up to 5 days, or frozen.

MAKES ABOUT 48 COOKIES

FROSTED FRUITS

To make frosted fruits, mix one egg white with a fork until frothy. Brush on desired fruits. Roll in sugar and set on a rack to dry. Use them within four hours.

BROWN SUGAR COOKIE DOUGH FOR CUTOUT COOKIES

These cookies add a different taste and color to your Christmas baking.

12 tablespoons (1½ sticks) butter or
    margarine, at room temperature
1½ cups firmly packed light brown sugar
1 large egg, at room temperature
1 tablespoon vanilla extract
3 cups all-purpose flour
½ teaspoon baking soda
1 teaspoon salt

✳ Cream the butter and brown sugar in a mixing bowl with an electric mixer until light and fluffy, about 2 minutes. Add the egg and vanilla extract, mixing for 2 minutes. Add the flour, baking soda, and salt, and mix until incorporated. Divide the dough into 3 parts. Flatten each into a disk and wrap in plastic wrap. Refrigerate until firm. Use as directed for Cutout Cookies (page 52).

The dough may be wrapped in plastic wrap and refrigerated for up to 5 days, or frozen.

MAKES ABOUT 48 COOKIES

BUTTER COOKIE DOUGH FOR CUTOUT COOKIES

This versatile dough makes very buttery, flaky cookies.

½ pound plus 2 tablespoons (2¼ sticks)
    butter or margarine, at room temperature
1 cup sugar
¼ teaspoon salt
3 egg yolks
1½ tablespoons whipping cream or
    half-and-half
½ teaspoons vanilla extract
3 cups all-purpose flour

✳ Cream the butter, sugar, and salt in a mixing bowl with an electric mixer until light and fluffy, about 2 minutes. Add the egg yolks, cream, and vanilla extract, and mix another 2 minutes. Add the flour and mix until incorporated. Divide the dough into 3 parts. Flatten each into a disk and wrap in plastic wrap. Refrigerate until firm. Use as directed for Cutout Cookies (page 52).

The dough may be wrapped in plastic wrap and refrigerated for up to 5 days, or frozen.

MAKES ABOUT 48 COOKIES

TO SOFTEN COOKIES

If soft cookies become dry and hard, they will soften if stored in an airtight container with something from which they can absorb moisture, such as a slice of fresh bread.

NO-BAKE GRANOLA BARS

So crunchy and chocolatey, these taste almost like a candy bar.

¼ pound (1 stick) butter or margarine
½ cup sugar
¼ cup unsweetened cocoa powder
1 large egg, at room temperature
1 teaspoon vanilla extract
2 cups granola without raisins
1 cup finely chopped walnuts

Vanilla Glaze
½ cup sifted powdered sugar
1 tablespoon milk

✳ Line an 8-inch square pan with foil, allowing the edges to extend over the rim of the pan.
✳ Melt the butter in a medium saucepan. Remove the pan from the heat. Whisk in the sugar, cocoa, and egg. Return to heat and stir constantly over low heat until the mixture is thick and smooth. Remove from the heat. Stir in the vanilla extract, granola, and nuts. Spoon the mixture into the lined pan, pressing evenly with the back of a spoon.
✳ To make the glaze, stir the powdered sugar and milk in a small bowl until smooth. Spread the glaze over the warm chocolate mixture and refrigerate until set, at least 2 hours. Remove from the pan by lifting on the foil. Place on a cutting surface and cut into 1½-inch squares. Refrigerate until ready to serve.

The cookies may be covered and refrigerated for up to 1 week, or frozen.

MAKES 25 BARS

CHOCOLATE CHIP-HAZELNUT SQUARES

These are simple to prepare and truly special. They are also great with pecans, walnuts, or almonds, if you wish to substitute them for the hazelnuts.

21 Oreo sandwich cookies
4 tablespoons (½ stick) butter or margarine
1¼ cups sweetened condensed milk
    (from a 14-ounce can)
1 cup (6 ounces) semisweet chocolate chips
1 cup peanut butter chips
1⅓ cups flaked coconut
1 cup (about 4 ounces) coarsely chopped
    hazelnuts, toasted (see Note on page 95)

✳ Preheat the oven to 350 degrees.
✳ Place the Oreos in a food processor fitted with the metal blade and process until ground into crumbs. You should have 2 cups of crumbs. Place the butter in a 9 x 13-inch baking pan and melt in the oven. Sprinkle the cookie crumbs over the butter; stir together with a spoon and press into the bottom of the pan. Drizzle 1 cup condensed milk evenly

over the crust. Layer chocolate chips, peanut butter chips, coconut, and nuts; press down firmly. Drizzle with the remaining ¼ cup condensed milk. Bake for 25 to 30 minutes, or until lightly browned. Cool to room temperature. Cut into 1½-inch squares.

The squares may be tightly covered and stored at room temperature for several days, or frozen. Defrost them, covered, at room temperature.

MAKES 48 SQUARES

Note: To toast hazelnuts, spread on an ungreased baking sheet and bake in a 350-degree oven until lightly browned, about 10 minutes.

WHITE CHOCOLATE HAYSTACKS

The heavenly harmony of sweet chocolate with salty peanuts and pretzels is an addicting combination.

12 ounces white chocolate, chopped
½ cup salted Spanish peanuts with skins
1½ cups thin pretzel sticks, broken into
 1½-inch pieces

❋ Line a baking sheet with waxed paper. Melt the white chocolate in the top of a double boiler over simmering water or in a medium bowl in the microwave on 60 percent power, stirring until smooth and creamy. Add the nuts and pretzels, stirring until well coated. Spoon the mixture by rounded teaspoonfuls onto the prepared baking sheet. Cool to room temperature or refrigerate.

❋ The cookies may be refrigerated indefinitely.

MAKES ABOUT 32 HAYSTACKS

FUDGE CRACKLES

These triple chocolate cookies with their cracked tops and fudgy interiors are great for mailing. They stay fresh a long time and are not fragile.

7 ounces semisweet chocolate, chopped
2 ounces unsweetened chocolate, chopped
3 tablespoons butter or margarine,
 at room temperature
1 cup sugar
3 large eggs, at room temperature
1 teaspoon vanilla extract
¾ cup all-purpose flour
½ teaspoon baking powder
¼ teaspoon salt
1 cup (6 ounces) semisweet chocolate chips
½ cup chopped walnuts

❋ Preheat the oven to 350 degrees. Grease 2 baking sheets. In a medium microwave-safe bowl or in a saucepan, melt both chocolates and butter, stirring until smooth. Cool slightly.

❋ Mix the sugar and eggs in a food processor fitted with the metal blade or in a mixing bowl with an electric mixer until thick and creamy. Mix in the vanilla extract and melted chocolate mixture. Add the flour, baking powder, and salt, and mix until incorporated. Add the chips and nuts and pulse 2 or 3 times or stir until mixed. Drop by teaspoonfuls about 1½ inches apart on the baking sheet. Bake for 8 minutes, or until the tops are cracked and shiny. Cool 3 to 5 minutes; remove to racks and cool completely.

The cookies may be stored in airtight containers at room temperature for up to several weeks, or frozen.

MAKES ABOUT 40 COOKIES

COOKIE WREATH

A beautiful way of serving cookies is to arrange them into a wreath. Make Butter, Chocolate, and Brown Sugar Cutout Cookies and decorate them with dark and white chocolate. Overlap them in circles on a large platter or board lined with fabric. Complete it with a big bow.

RASPBERRY MERINGUE BARS

One batch of these elegant cookies will fill lots of tins for Christmas giving. For chocolate lovers, sprinkle 1 cup miniature chocolate chips over the jam before topping with the meringue.

Pastry
½ pound (2 sticks) butter or margarine,
 at room temperature
½ cup sugar
2 egg yolks
2½ cups all-purpose flour

Topping
1 jar (10 ounces) seedless raspberry jam
4 egg whites, at room temperature
¼ teaspoon salt
1 cup sugar
2 cups finely chopped walnuts

❋ Preheat the oven to 350 degrees. Grease a 15½ x 10½ x 1-inch jelly-roll pan.

❋ To make the pastry, cream the butter, sugar, and egg yolks in a food processor fitted with the metal blade or in a mixing bowl with an electric mixer until well blended. Add the flour and mix until incorporated. Pat the dough into the bottom of the prepared pan. Bake for 15 to 20 minutes, or until lightly browned. Remove from the oven, but leave the oven at 350 degrees.

✳ Cool the pastry for 5 minutes, then spread it with jam. Beat the egg whites and salt in a mixing bowl with an electric mixer until stiff, but not dry, peaks form. Fold in the sugar and the nuts. Gently spread meringue on top of the jam, making sure to seal the edges and corners. Return to the oven for 25 minutes, or until golden brown. While still warm, cut into 3 x 1-inch bars.

The cookies may be stored in airtight containers at room temperature for up to 1 week, or frozen. Defrost them, covered, at room temperature.

MAKES 50 BARS

GRAND MARNIER BROWNIES

This sophisticated adult brownie has just enough Grand Marnier in it to remind us that orange and chocolate are an unbeatable combination.

4 ounces unsweetened chocolate, chopped
¼ pound (1 stick) butter or margarine
¾ cup firmly packed dark brown sugar
¾ cup granulated sugar
2 large eggs, at room temperature
4 tablespoons Grand Marnier, divided
1 teaspoon vanilla extract
1 teaspoon grated orange peel
¾ cup all-purpose flour
⅛ teaspoon salt
½ cup (3 ounces) semisweet chocolate chips

✳ Preheat the oven to 350 degrees. Grease and flour an 8-inch square pan. Melt the chocolate and butter in a medium saucepan over low heat, stirring until smooth. Remove from the heat and cool slightly. Beat the brown and granulated sugars and the eggs in a large bowl with an electric mixer until light and fluffy, about 2 minutes. Add the melted chocolate mixture, 3 tablespoons of the Grand Marnier, the vanilla extract and orange peel, mixing until blended. Mix in the flour, salt, and chocolate chips on low speed. Pour the mixture into the prepared pan and smooth the top. Bake 30 to 35 minutes, or until the sides look done and the top feels firm. A cake tester inserted 2 inches from the center should test clean, but the center will jiggle and look undercooked. Remove from the oven and brush the top with the remaining 1 tablespoon Grand Marnier. Cover the pan with plastic wrap and cool completely. Cut into 2-inch squares.

The brownies may be covered and stored at room temperature for up to several days, or frozen. Defrost them, covered, at room temperature.

MAKES 16 BROWNIES

WRAPPING THEM UP
To give cookies as gifts, fill containers you have around the house. Empty oatmeal boxes, coffee tins, and ice cream containers can be lined with waxed paper and covered with Christmas wrap. Small baskets, strawberry baskets, and decorated paper bags are also good choices.

CANDIES AND CONFECTIONS

COFFEE MERINGUE NUTS

Although pecans work beautifully in this recipe, almonds, cashews, and walnuts are delicious as well.

4 tablespoons (½ stick) butter or margarine, melted
1 pound pecan halves
1⅓ cups sugar
1 teaspoon ground cinnamon
2 tablespoons instant coffee granules
2 large egg whites, at room temperature

✳ Preheat the oven to 300 degrees. Pour the melted butter over the nuts in a bowl and toss well. Combine ⅔ cup of the sugar, cinnamon, and coffee granules in a small bowl. Sprinkle over the nuts and stir, coating the nuts as evenly as possible. Beat the egg whites in the small bowl of an electric mixer until soft peaks form. Gradually add the remaining ⅔ cup sugar, beating until stiff peaks form. Fold the nut mixture into the egg whites. Spread the mixture on a rimmed baking sheet. Bake for 25 to 30 minutes, stirring every 10 minutes. Cool to room temperature. Store in tightly sealed jars in the refrigerator.

The nuts may be covered and refrigerated for up to 6 months.

MAKES 1 POUND

FLORENTINE TOFFEE

Combine butter, sugar, honey, and cream. Stir in nuts and bake in aluminum pie dishes, tartlet pans, or muffin cups, and voilà! you have a confection that is round and crisp like a cookie, but buttery and crunchy like toffee. A beautiful gift.

½ pound (2 sticks) unsalted butter
1 cup sugar
⅓ cup honey
⅓ cup whipping cream
16 ounces (4 cups) sliced almonds, or 8 ounces (2 cups) almonds and 8 ounces (2 cups) chopped pecans
8 ounces semisweet chocolate, melted (optional)

✳ Preheat the oven to 375 degrees. Butter 5 eight-inch aluminum pie pans, or 29 two-inch muffin cups or tartlet pans. Combine the butter, sugar, honey, and cream in a heavy, deep saucepan. Bring to a boil over moderate heat, stirring frequently. When the mixture

comes to a boil, cook, stirring constantly, for 1½ minutes. Remove from heat and stir in the nuts.

✳ Divide the mixture among the pans, using a rounded soup spoon to fill the muffin tins. Pat the mixture evenly into the bottom of the pans, using a spoon or your fingers dipped in cold water. The pans should be filled about ½ inch deep. Bake for 8 to 12 minutes, or until golden brown. Timing will depend on the type of pans used. This step may be done in batches, if necessary. Remove the pans from the oven and cool slightly. Refrigerate 5 to 10 minutes, or until just firm enough to go around the edges with the tip of a sharp knife. Remove them to waxed paper. Cool completely.

✳ If desired, spread melted chocolate on the flat sides of the candies. Refrigerate until the chocolate is hardened.

The candy may be stored in a cool place in an airtight container for up to 1 month, or refrigerated indefinitely.

MAKES TWENTY NINE 2-INCH OR FIVE 8-INCH CANDIES

CANDY BAR DOUBLE-NUT FUDGE

This fudge is proof that the best can also be the easiest.

2 cups sugar
½ teaspoon salt
4 tablespoons (½ stick) butter or margarine
1 can (5 ounces) evaporated milk
1 package (12 ounces) semisweet
    chocolate chips
1 bar (8 ounces) milk chocolate with almonds
1 jar (7 ounces) marshmallow creme
2 teaspoons vanilla extract
2 cups (about 8 ounces) coarsely chopped
    walnuts or pecans

✳ Heavily butter a 9 x 13-inch baking pan; set aside. Place the sugar, salt, butter, and evaporated milk in a large, heavy saucepan. Bring to a boil over moderately high heat, stirring constantly.

✳ When the mixture comes to a boil, lower the heat to medium. Boil gently for 8 to 9 minutes, stirring frequently to make sure the bottom doesn't scorch. Stir in the chocolate chips, chocolate bar, and marshmallow creme until the chocolate is melted and the mixture is well blended. Stir in the vanilla extract and nuts. Pour the mixture into the prepared pan. Cool at room temperature for several hours, or until set. Cut into 1-inch squares.

The fudge may be stored in an airtight container at room temperature for up to 2 weeks, refrigerated for up to 1 month, or frozen for up to 6 months.

MAKES 117 PIECES

ABOUT TRUFFLES
Chocolate truffles, which are so named because they resemble the prized woodland mushroom (in looks only), are simply a confection made with chocolate, heavy cream, and flavoring. They can be rolled or piped and then coated as desired. To cover with melted chocolate, insert a toothpick into the truffle, dip until completely covered and stick into a piece of Styrofoam to harden.

TO MAKE A HARVEST WREATH
Choose an 18- to 20-inch straw-based wreath. Insert Christmas evergreen, pine, or rosemary sparsely around the wreath. To attach vegetables, use floral picks. Press a wireless pick into soft vegetables and fruits. Use picks with wire to wrap around hard items such as gourds and garlic, nuts and pods. Fill in spaces with additional greens.

CHOCOLATE TRUFFLES
Truffles, intensely rich chocolate confections, can be presented in two different shapes. They may be formed into balls and rolled in cocoa, sprinkles, or chocolate, or piped through a pastry bag onto waxed paper.

4 ounces unsweetened chocolate, chopped
4 ounces semisweet chocolate, chopped
⅓ cup water
12 tablespoons (1½ sticks) butter or
    margarine, at room temperature
2 cups powdered sugar, sifted
1 large egg yolk, at room temperature
2 tablespoons rum
Unsweetened cocoa powder, chocolate
    sprinkles, melted or chopped chocolate,
    for garnish

✳ Place both chocolates and water in a medium saucepan, and melt over low heat, stirring constantly. Cool to room temperature. Mix the butter, powdered sugar, egg yolk, and rum in a mixing bowl with an electric mixer until light and fluffy. Mix in the melted chocolate mixture. To make rosettes, line a baking sheet with waxed paper or bonbon papers. Spoon the truffle mixture into a pastry bag fitted with a large (1¼-inch) star or rosette tip. Pipe a large rosette onto the paper or into each cup and refrigerate or freeze until set.

✳ To shape into balls, refrigerate the truffle mixture until firm enough to roll into ¾-inch balls. Roll the balls in cocoa, sprinkles, or finely chopped chocolate or dip in melted chocolate to cover. Refrigerate or freeze until firm.

The truffles may be stored in an airtight container in the refrigerator for up to 3 weeks, or frozen. Serve chilled.

MAKES ABOUT 50 TRUFFLES

CELEBRATING THE NEW YEAR

ANOTHER YEAR

The year is gone,

    It's slipped away

So much more to do

    So much more to say.

But keep the hope,

    It's not too late

To have a party

    And celebrate.

Pop the cork,

    Pour the champagne

When midnight strikes

    We begin again.

Marlene Sorosky

N EW YEAR'S *marks not only the end of the year, but the end of the holiday season. It's a natural time to be nostalgic and reminisce, as well as to anticipate and welcome a fresh start. This occasion offers two completely different styles of entertaining. The mood can be either sophisticated and elegant or casual and carefree. For this chapter I have chosen the less formal of the two. If you prefer a black-tie celebration, begin your evening with champagne and caviar and follow it with Perfect Prime Rib Roast (page 83) and Butter Lettuce Salad with Dried Cranberries and Oranges (page 70). A grand finale fitting for this occasion is the Chocolate Mousse Ice Cream Ball (page 75), substituting Jamoca Almond Fudge ice cream for the pink peppermint.*

A MIDNIGHT MADNESS BUFFET

Assorted Appetizers

A VEGETABLE FLOWER BASKET

ROASTED RED BELL PEPPER DIP (PAGE 65)

TAMALE TARTLETS (PAGES 58-59)

OVEN-FRIED SESAME EGGPLANT (PAGE 57)

Main Dishes

SOUTH OF THE BORDER SALAD

CHICKEN CHILI

CORN SPOONBREAD CASSEROLE

BAKED TOMATO MACARONI

Dessert

ROCKY ROAD COLA BARS

ASSORTED APPETIZERS

A VEGETABLE FLOWER BASKET

Choose a low basket that is a suitable size for your table. Line the basket with Napa or Savoy cabbage leaves. Prepare the vegetables as directed. Fill the basket with the desired vegetables as close to serving time as possible. Spray the vegetables with water as often as possible after assembling to keep them fresh until your guests arrive. Serve the basket with Roasted Red Bell Pepper Dip or other desired dip.

Leek Flowers

❋ For each flower, choose the largest leek possible. It must be at least 1 inch in diameter. Wash the leek. Cut off the top, leaving approximately a 4-inch stalk. Cut a thin slice off the root end so it stands flat. Cut in half lengthwise, going only halfway down to the root. Then cut into quarters, sixths, or eighths, depending on the size of the leek, cutting only halfway down toward the root. As close to serving time as possible, peel back the first ribbonlike layer and fold it into itself, forming a loop. Continue folding each row, working from the bottom up, until the layers become so brittle you can't fold anymore. Continue in the same manner, working around the leek. Keep in ice water until ready to use. Place on a skewer and insert in the basket.

Red Cabbage Hibiscus

❋ Cut a red cabbage in half. Carefully tear off leaves. Cut out 3 petals per flower. Fringe the edges with scissors. Make green onion brushes by cutting a 2-inch piece of green onion from the root end. Cut the root flat. Make very thin slices, cutting down from the top, leaving the bottom ½ inch intact. Put into ice water for several hours or overnight to open out. Place 3 cabbage leaves on skewers. Place a green onion brush in the center. Leave in ice water until ready to assemble the basket.

Daikon Daisies

❋ Peel a daikon radish and slice on the diagonal as thin as possible. Put in ice water overnight for the edges to curl. Peel carrots. Cut and taper the top, making about a 1½-inch stamen. Place 4 or 5 daikon petals on skewers. Place the carrot stamen in the center. Keep in ice water until ready to assemble the basket.

MAIN DISHES

SOUTH OF THE BORDER SALAD

Everyone's favorite Mexican flavors are tossed into this tostada-like taco salad.

2 cans (2.2 ounces each) sliced black olives
1 can (16 ounces) red kidney beans
1 can (16 ounces) garbanzo beans
2 medium heads iceberg lettuce, washed and torn into bite-sized pieces
2 bunches green onions, chopped
4 medium tomatoes, chopped
2 avocados, sliced
1 pound sharp Cheddar cheese, shredded (about 4 cups)
2 bags (½ pound each) tortilla or taco chips
⅔ cup mild salsa
6 tablespoons bottled Thousand Island dressing

❋ Drain olives and beans in a colander. Toss the lettuce, green onions, olives, kidney and garbanzo beans, tomatoes, avocados, cheese, and tortilla chips in a large salad bowl. Combine the salsa and dressing in a small bowl. Pour over the salad and toss well. Serve immediately.

SERVES 16

CHICKEN CHILI

Is the best chili made with or without beans? This question has been highly debated in the great chili controversy. Now we can add a second question. Is chili best made with chicken, beef, or pork? You'll have to try this tasty version and decide for yourself.

6 whole chicken breasts, split (about 7 to 8 pounds)
Salt and black pepper

4 large onions, chopped

10 large cloves garlic, finely minced

4 tablespoons vegetable oil

4 cans or bottles (12 ounces each) beer

4 teaspoons dried oregano

½ cup chili powder, or to taste

4 tablespoons ground cumin

12 chicken bouillon cubes

½ cup water

2 teaspoons whole coriander seeds (optional)

2 cans (15 ounces each) tomato sauce

2 cans (16 ounces each) kidney beans,
    drained (optional)

1 can (16 ounces) pinto beans,
    drained (optional)

Condiments (optional)

2 to 3 cups shredded sharp Cheddar cheese

2 cans (4 ounces each) sliced black olives,
    drained

2 onions, chopped

2 to 3 bunches fresh cilantro, chopped

4 to 6 tomatoes, chopped

2 cups sour cream

✳ To poach the chicken, preheat the oven to 350 degrees. Sprinkle the chicken with salt and pepper. Place it, skin-side up, in a shallow pan and add ½ inch water. Cover with a buttered sheet of waxed paper, buttered-side down, tucking in the edges of the paper. Bake for 20 to 30 minutes, or until the meat near the bone is barely pink. Remove the chicken from the oven and cool to room temperature. Remove skin and bones and cut or tear meat into 1-inch pieces. Set aside.

✳ In a large wide nonaluminum pot, sauté the onions and garlic in oil until soft. Add the beer, oregano, chili powder, cumin, bouillon cubes, water, coriander seeds, if using, and tomato sauce. Bring to a boil over moderately

high heat, reduce the heat to low, and simmer, uncovered, for 1½ hours, stirring occasionally. Stir in the beans, if using, and simmer 30 more minutes. Stir in the reserved chicken.

The chili may be cooled, then well covered and refrigerated overnight, or frozen. Defrost it at room temperature.

✳ Before serving, simmer the chili 15 minutes, or until heated through, stirring occasionally. Serve with the assorted condiments, as desired.

SERVES 12

CORN SPOONBREAD CASSEROLE

As this casserole bakes, it magically separates into layers. The top and bottom become moist corn bread, sandwiching a creamy custard filling.

2 cups yellow cornmeal

1⅓ cups all-purpose flour

6 tablespoons sugar

1 teaspoon salt

2 teaspoons baking soda

2 teaspoons baking powder

2½ cups milk

2½ cups whole, low-fat, or nonfat buttermilk

4 large eggs, at room temperature

1 can (17 ounces) creamed corn, undrained

3 tablespoons salsa jalapeña or ¼ teaspoon
    Tabasco sauce

4 tablespoons (½ stick) butter or margarine

✳ Preheat the oven to 400 degrees.

✳ In a large bowl, stir together the cornmeal, flour, sugar, salt, baking soda, and baking powder. Stir in 1½ cups of the milk and 1½ cups of the buttermilk. Whisk in the eggs until blended. Stir in the creamed corn and salsa or Tabasco. Place the butter in a 9 x 13-

inch glass casserole dish. Place in the oven until the butter is melted, 2 to 3 minutes. Pour the batter into the hot dish and carefully pour the remaining 1 cup milk and 1 cup buttermilk over the batter. Do not stir. Bake for 30 to 40 minutes, or until puffed and golden brown and the top feels firm. Remove from the oven and cool 10 to 15 minutes before serving.

The casserole may be covered and refrigerated overnight, or frozen. Defrost it at room temperature. Reheat at 350 degrees for 10 minutes, or until heated through.

✳ To serve, cut into about 3-inch squares.

SERVES 12

BAKED TOMATO MACARONI

No, there is not a mistake in this recipe. The pasta actually bakes without being boiled first. Be generous with your seasonings and garlic, as baking reduces their pungency. You can make several batches of this crowd-pleaser and reheat it, but don't try doubling the recipe in one pan.

1 pound uncooked large elbow macaroni,
    mostaccioli, or penne

½ cup extra-virgin olive oil

9 to 12 garlic cloves, minced

1 cup chopped onion

1 tablespoon sugar

1 teaspoon crushed dried red chili pepper

¼ cup dried basil, crumbled

2 tablespoons dried oregano, crumbled

3 cans (1 pound 12 ounces each) tomatoes,
    undrained

Grated Parmesan cheese, for serving

✳ Place the pasta in a large bowl. Pour the olive oil over the pasta, toss well, and let sit for 1 hour. Pour pasta into a strainer and drain off excess oil into a deep nonaluminum saucepan. Add the garlic, onion, sugar, chili pepper, basil, and oregano to oil. Heat over moderate heat until the oil gets very hot, about 10 minutes. Remove from the heat and cool to room temperature. Crush the tomatoes with your hands or a food processor fitted with the metal blade and add them and their liquid to the oil mixture in the saucepan.

❋ Preheat the oven to 400 degrees. Place the drained pasta in a large nonaluminum roasting pan; pour the room temperature sauce over the pasta and stir well. Bake, uncovered, in the center of the oven for 40 minutes, turning with a spatula every 10 minutes to ensure that all the pasta cooks evenly.

❋ Serve with Parmesan cheese.

MAKES 12 SIDE-DISH OR 8 MAIN-DISH SERVINGS

DESSERT

ROCKY ROAD COLA BARS

I don't know why, but soda pop helps tenderize this moist chocolate cake and intensify its sweet flavor. Miniature marshmallows and nuts, stirred into the fudgy frosting, add decadence to indulgence.

Chocolate Cola Cake
2 cups all-purpose flour
2 cups sugar
4 tablespoons unsweetened cocoa powder
½ teaspoon salt
½ pound (2 sticks) butter or margarine, at room temperature, cut into small pieces
1 cup cola
2 large eggs, at room temperature
½ cup buttermilk

1 teaspoon baking soda
1 teaspoon vanilla extract

Rocky Road Cola Frosting
¼ pound (1 stick) butter or margarine
⅓ cup cola
1 teaspoon instant coffee granules
2 tablespoons water
1 pound powdered sugar, sifted
5 tablespoons unsweetened cocoa powder
1 cup (about 4 ounces) chopped walnuts
1½ cups miniature marshmallows

❋ To make the cake, grease and flour a 9 x 13-inch baking pan; set aside. Preheat the oven to 350 degrees. Stir together the flour, sugar, cocoa, and salt in a large bowl. Bring the butter and cola to a boil in a small saucepan. Pour the butter mixture over the flour mixture and stir with a wooden spoon until combined. Whisk the eggs in a medium bowl until frothy. Add buttermilk, baking soda, and vanilla extract to eggs, and whisk until blended. Stir the egg mixture into the batter until incorporated. The batter will be thin. Pour into the prepared pan. Bake for 30 minutes, or until a cake tester inserted in the center comes out clean.

❋ While the cake bakes, make the frosting. Bring the butter, cola, coffee granules, and water to a boil in a small saucepan. Stir the powdered sugar and cocoa together in a medium bowl. Pour the butter-cola mixture over the sugar mixture; stir with a wooden spoon until well blended. Fold in the walnuts and marshmallows.

❋ Remove the cake from the oven and pour the frosting over the top of the hot cake, spreading to the sides of the pan. Cool to room temperature.

The cake may be tightly covered and kept at room temperature for up to one week, or frozen. Defrost it at room temperature.
❋ Before serving, cut into 1½-inch squares.

MAKES ABOUT 48 BARS

NEW YEAR'S DECOR
New Year's does not have the symbolism of many other holidays, so you need to be more creative in your decorating. Bring out all forms of timepieces: watches, clocks, and hourglasses. Set the clocks for midnight, drape them with streamers, and sprinkle the table with confetti.

A NEW YEAR'S DAY BRUNCH

UPSIDE-DOWN SAUSAGE-APPLE CORN BREAD

SCRAMBLED EGGS WITH GOAT CHEESE

HERBED CREAM PUFF BOWL

PUFFED EGGNOG PANCAKE

MAPLE-GLAZED BACON

UPSIDE-DOWN SAUSAGE-APPLE CORN BREAD

Corn bread has never looked so good or tasted better. It's baked atop rows of brown sugar-glazed sausage links and sautéed apple slices and then inverted. It makes a truly spectacular breakfast entree.

½ pound pork sausage links
4 tablespoons (½ stick) butter or margarine
½ cup packed light brown sugar
4 small apples, peeled and cut into eighths
Maple syrup, for serving

Corn Bread

1 cup all-purpose flour

¾ cup yellow cornmeal

3 tablespoons packed light brown sugar

1 tablespoon baking powder

1 teaspoon salt

1 large egg, lightly beaten

4 tablespoons (½ stick) butter or margarine, melted

1 cup milk

✳ Grease the bottom and sides of an 8 x 2- or 9 x 2-inch square pan. Brown the sausages in a medium skillet over moderately high heat, rotating them until browned and cooked through. Remove the sausages and discard all but 2 tablespoons drippings. Add the butter and brown sugar to the skillet. Heat, stirring, until the sugar is melted. Add the apples and sauté them over moderate heat, turning occasionally, until soft, about 10 minutes.

✳ Arrange the sausages in rows across the bottom of the prepared pan. Insert the apple slices, rounded-sides down, between the rows of sausage, wedging them in tightly. Pour pan juices over sausages.

The pan may be covered and refrigerated overnight at this point.

✳ Preheat the oven to 400 degrees. To make the corn bread, stir the flour, cornmeal, brown sugar, baking powder, and salt in a medium bowl. Add the egg, melted butter, and milk, and stir with a wooden spoon until well combined. Pour the batter over the apples and sausages, smoothing the top to cover well. Bake for 20 to 25 minutes, or until a cake tester inserted into the bread comes out clean. Remove from the oven and immediately invert onto a platter. Serve in squares with maple syrup.

SERVES 6 TO 8

SCRAMBLED EGGS WITH GOAT CHEESE

Wait until you taste these. Goat cheese does something magical to eggs.

3 tablespoons butter or margarine

9 eggs

3½ to 4 ounces goat cheese

1 recipe Herbed Cream Puff Bowl (optional; recipe follows)

✳ Melt the butter in a large skillet over moderate heat. Whisk the eggs in a medium bowl until well blended. Pour the eggs into the skillet. Crumble or cut the cheese into small pieces and sprinkle over the eggs. Stir gently with a wooden spoon until the eggs are just set but still soft. Serve immediately, in an herbed cream puff bowl, if desired.

SERVES 6

HERBED CREAM PUFF BOWL

The perfect holder for eggs, this fancy but easy-to-make "bowl" takes the place of toast.

¾ cup water

6 tablespoons (¾ stick) butter or margarine, at room temperature, cut into 6 pieces

¼ teaspoon salt

¾ teaspoon dried thyme, crumbled

¾ teaspoon dried oregano, crumbled

1½ teaspoons dried basil, crumbled

¾ cup all-purpose flour

3 large eggs, at room temperature

Scrambled eggs

✳ Preheat the oven to 400 degrees. Butter the sides and bottom of a 9-inch pie plate. Bring the water, butter, salt, thyme, oregano, and basil to a boil in a medium saucepan, stirring to melt the butter. Add the flour all at once, stirring vigorously with a wooden spoon to incorporate it. Remove from the heat and cool 5 minutes. Beat in the eggs, one at a time, mixing with an electric hand mixer in the saucepan or with an electric mixer in a mixing bowl until the dough is smooth and shiny. Pour the dough into the pie plate. Freeze 5 to 10 minutes to firm it up slightly. Spread a thin layer of dough on the bottom and up the sides of the dish; it will be stiff.

The pastry may be frozen at this point. Defrost it at room temperature for 3 hours before baking.

✳ Bake for 35 to 40 minutes, or until the bowl is puffed and golden. Remove it to a platter and fill with scrambled eggs. Cut into wedges to serve.

SERVES 6

PUFFED EGGNOG PANCAKE

This holiday pancake needs lots of space in the oven to reach its high, glorious volume, so be sure to bake it on the middle or lower rack.

6 eggs

1⅓ cups eggnog

1 cup all-purpose flour

¾ teaspoon ground nutmeg

¼ pound (1 stick) butter or margarine

½ cup sliced almonds

1 tablespoon sugar

Fruit-flavored pancake syrup, such as blueberry, boysenberry, or strawberry, for serving

✳ Preheat the oven to 425 degrees. Mix the eggs in a large mixing bowl with an electric mixer or a food processor with the metal blade. Add the eggnog, flour, and nutmeg and mix until well blended. The batter will be slightly lumpy. Place the butter in a 9 x 13-inch glass baking dish and place it in the oven until the butter is melted and sizzling; do not let it brown. Remove pan from oven and immediately pour the batter into the pan.

Rocky Road Cola Bars, page 107

Sprinkle the top with almonds and sugar. Return the pan to the oven and bake for 15 to 20 minutes, or until puffed and browned. Serve immediately with the syrup.

SERVES 6

MAPLE-GLAZED BACON

This crisp maple-candied bacon is absolutely irresistible. It can be made ahead and reheated when you are ready to serve.

1 pound thickly sliced bacon
½ cup maple syrup
1 teaspoon dry mustard

❋ Preheat the oven to 400 degrees. Line a shallow-rimmed baking sheet or broiler pan with heavy foil. Place a rack in the pan and arrange the bacon on the rack. Whisk the maple syrup and mustard together in a small bowl. Brush over the top of the bacon. Bake for 15 minutes. Turn the bacon over and brush again with syrup mixture. Bake an additional 5 to 10 minutes, or until the bacon is very crisp and golden. Remove the pan from the oven and let the bacon rest on the rack for 5 minutes, then loosen. Do not drain on paper towels as the bacon will stick.

The bacon may be wrapped in foil and refrigerated, or frozen. Reheat on the rack at 400 degrees for 5 minutes.

MAKES ABOUT 12 SLICES; SERVES 5 OR 6

Here's to champagne, the drink divine
That makes us forget our troubles;
It's made of a dollar's worth of wine
And three dollars' worth of bubbles.

Anonymous

MUNCHY FOOD FOR TV FANS

BLOODY MARY PUNCH
(PAGE 87)

CONFETTI SALSA
WITH CHIPS

ITALIAN SAUSAGE SOUP

HOT AND CRUSTY SHRIMP
SANDWICH

GREEN BEAN, FENNEL, AND
WALNUT SALAD

CRUNCHY CHINESE
CABBAGE SALAD

FROZEN OREO FUDGE
SQUARES

CONFETTI SALSA

Bits of tomatoes, carrots, corn, and avocado make a chunky salsa that resembles confetti. Serve it with chips or slices of cucumber or jícama.

2 cloves garlic, peeled
1 small pickled or fresh jalapeño
 (¾ to 1 inch), seeded
1 medium carrot, peeled and cut into
 1-inch pieces
½ medium onion, quartered
2 medium tomatoes, seeded and very
 coarsely chopped
½ cup corn kernels
2 tablespoons finely chopped fresh cilantro
2 tablespoons fresh lemon juice
1 medium avocado, peeled and cut into
 ½-inch pieces
Salt and black pepper
Tortilla chips and/or sliced cucumber
 and jícama

❋ In a food processor with the metal blade, process garlic and jalapeño until finely

---

minced. Add carrot and onion and pulse until finely chopped. Remove to a medium bowl. Pulse tomatoes until finely chopped. Add to carrot mixture in bowl. Stir in corn, cilantro, and lemon juice.

The salsa may be covered and refrigerated overnight.

❋ Before serving, drain off excess liquid. Stir in avocado. Season with salt and pepper to taste. Serve with chips or vegetables.

MAKES 3 CUPS

ITALIAN SAUSAGE SOUP

Unmistakably Italian with its sausage, red wine, basil, and spaghetti, this complete meal in a bowl will be popular with family and friends throughout the winter months.

1 pound mild or hot Italian sausage
2 tablespoons vegetable oil
2 onions, chopped
2 cloves garlic, minced
1 can (28 ounces) whole tomatoes, undrained
3 tablespoons tomato paste
7 cups beef broth
1 cup dry red wine
2 tablespoons dried basil
2 teaspoons dried oregano
2 medium zucchini, thinly sliced
½ cup chopped fresh parsley
5 ounces uncooked thin spaghetti,
 broken into 2-inch pieces
1 can (1 pound) garbanzo beans, drained
Salt and black pepper
Grated Parmesan cheese, for serving

❋ Slice sausage into ¼-inch-thick rounds. Place them in a large skillet and sauté until lightly browned. Remove with a slotted

Scrambled Eggs with Goat Cheese in Herbed Cream Puff Bowl, page 109

spoon to a large soup pot. Add the vegetable oil to the drippings in the skillet and sauté the onions and garlic until soft. Remove with slotted spoon to the soup pot. Add the tomatoes with their liquid, tomato paste, broth, red wine, basil, and oregano. Cook, uncovered, over moderate heat for 30 minutes, stirring occasionally. Add the zucchini, parsley, and spaghetti. Continue cooking, stirring occasionally, until spaghetti is tender, about 20 to 30 minutes. Add the garbanzo beans for the last 10 minutes of cooking. Season with salt and pepper to taste.

The soup may be refrigerated for several days, or frozen.

✳ Serve with Parmesan cheese.

MAKES 6 TO 8 MAIN-DISH SERVINGS

HOT AND CRUSTY SHRIMP SANDWICH

Half a loaf of French bread is scooped out, then filled with layers of marinated shrimp, red onions, olives, and pimiento. It's then baked until the shrimp are cooked and juicy and the bread is golden and toasty. Inspired by fireman chef Jim Neil, this colorful shrimp sandwich is delicious hot or at room temperature.

Marinade

2 tablespoons vegetable oil
1 clove garlic, minced
2 teaspoons dry mustard
1 teaspoon salt
¼ cup lemon juice
2 teaspoons red wine vinegar
Dash of cayenne pepper

Sandwich

½ medium red onion, thinly sliced
½ pound large raw shrimp, peeled and deveined
1 loaf (1 pound) French bread, cut in half horizontally (reserve the other half for Puffed Turkey Sandwich Loaf, page 37)
6 tablespoons (¾ stick) butter or margarine, at room temperature
5 tablespoons chopped fresh parsley
4 cloves garlic, minced
3 tablespoons sliced black olives
3 tablespoons chopped pimiento

✳ To make the marinade, mix the oil, garlic, mustard, salt, lemon juice, vinegar, and cayenne in a medium glass or plastic bowl. Stir in the sliced onion and shrimp. Cover and marinate in the refrigerator up to 3 hours.

✳ Using your hands, remove as much bread as possible from the inside of the half-loaf of French bread, leaving a 1-inch rim. Place the bread pieces in a food processor fitted with the metal blade and process into crumbs; measure 1 cup. Sauté the 1 cup crumbs in 2 tablespoons of the butter until golden; set aside.

✳ Preheat the oven to 400 degrees. With a fork, mix the remaining 4 tablespoons butter with 3 tablespoons of the parsley and the garlic in a small bowl until combined. Spread on the bottom and top edges of the hollowed loaf. Remove the shrimp and onions from the marinade and place in the loaf. Sprinkle with the olives and pimiento. Drizzle with 3 tablespoons of the marinade. (Discard remaining marinade.) Sprinkle with the sautéed bread crumbs and remaining 2 tablespoons parsley.

✳ Place the bread on a sheet of foil in the center of the oven. Bake for 18 to 20 minutes,

or until the shrimp are pink and the bread is crusty. Cut into 6 slices to serve. Serve warm or at room temperature.

MAKES SIX SANDWICHES

GREEN BEAN, FENNEL, AND WALNUT SALAD

Dill sparks up the flavor of an aromatic walnut oil vinaigrette. Store walnut oil in the refrigerator after opening it.

2 pounds green beans, ends trimmed, cut into 3- and 4-inch lengths
1 tablespoon salt
2 small or 1 large fennel bulb (about 1½ pounds)

Walnut-Dill Dressing

2 tablespoons raspberry vinegar
¼ cup orange juice
1 teaspoon Dijon mustard
¼ cup walnut oil
½ cup fresh chopped dill or 2 tablespoons dried dill

½ cup coarsely chopped walnuts, toasted (see Note, page 113)

✳ Trim, rinse, and drain the beans. Fill a large soup pot three quarters full of water. Add salt and bring to a boil. Add the beans and cook them until they are tender to the bite, about 5 to 7 minutes. Drain and immediately run them under cold water to stop the cooking. Pat dry and transfer to a bowl. Meanwhile, cut a thin slice off the top and root end of the fennel and discard. Slice the bulb into ¼-inch slices and then into 2-inch pieces. Add the fennel to the beans, cover, and refrigerate until chilled or overnight.

* To make the dressing, whisk the vinegar, orange juice, and mustard in a small bowl. Whisk in the walnut oil until blended. Stir in the dill.

The dressing may be refrigerated for several days.

* Up to 6 hours before serving, pour the dressing over the beans. Refrigerate until serving. Immediately before serving, add the toasted chopped walnuts and toss.

SERVES 8 TO 10

Note: To toast walnuts, spread on an ungreased baking sheet and bake in a 350-degree oven until lightly browned, about 10 minutes.

CRUNCHY CHINESE CABBAGE SALAD

Whether I'm going on a picnic, having friends over to watch a game, or bringing a dish to a potluck, this sturdy and popular salad is often my first choice. I am partial to its sweet and tangy oriental dressing enhanced with slivers of toasted almonds and crisp noodles.

Salad

1 head Napa cabbage (about 2½ pounds)
¼ small head red cabbage
1 cup sliced green onion with tops
     (about 2 bunches)
2 tablespoons butter or margarine
1 cup (4 ounces) slivered almonds
¼ cup (1 ounce) sesame seeds
1 package Ramen noodles, crushed
     (do not use flavoring packet)

Dressing

⅓ cup seasoned rice vinegar
½ cup vegetable oil
⅓ cup sugar
3 tablespoons soy sauce

* Tear off outer leaves from Napa cabbage and reserve to line salad bowl, if desired. Cut out the core and slice the cabbage into 1-inch strips. Cut slices into 1-inch pieces. Remove core from red cabbage and cut into 1-inch pieces. Put cabbage and green onions in a large bowl. Refrigerate.

* In a medium skillet over moderately high heat, melt the butter. Sauté the almonds, sesame seeds, and noodles until golden, stirring frequently. Cool completely.

* To make the dressing, in a bowl or jar, mix vinegar, oil, sugar, and soy sauce.

Cabbage and dressing may be refrigerated separately overnight.

* If desired, line salad bowl with Napa cabbage leaves. Pour dressing over cabbage and green onions. Add nut mixture and toss well. Place in salad bowl and serve immediately.

MAKES 8 TO 10 SERVINGS

FROZEN OREO FUDGE SQUARES

Sink your teeth through three chocolate layers—creamy fudge, ice cream, and crushed Oreo cookies. Store this dessert in your freezer so it is ready whenever your guests are.

30 Oreo sandwich cookies
6 tablespoons (¾ stick) butter or margarine,
     melted
½ gallon chocolate almond or chocolate–
     chocolate chip ice cream
3 ounces unsweetened chocolate

¼ pound (1 stick) butter or margarine,
     cut into 4 pieces
2 cups powdered sugar
4 eggs, separated

* Place the cookies in the container of a food processor fitted with the metal blade and process until they are reduced to fine crumbs. Add 6 tablespoons melted butter to cookie crumbs and mix until combined. Press 2 cups of the crumb mixture over the bottom of a 9 x 13-inch baking pan. Soften the ice cream slightly and spread over the crumb layer. Freeze until firm.

* Meanwhile, melt the chocolate and ¼ pound butter in a medium saucepan over low heat. Remove from the heat and stir in the powdered sugar. The mixture will be very stiff. Whisk egg whites in a medium bowl until blended and stir into the chocolate mixture. In a mixing bowl with an electric mixer, beat egg whites until soft peaks form. Fold a dollop of egg whites into the chocolate mixture to lighten it and then fold in the rest until thoroughly combined. Spread over the ice cream. Sprinkle the remaining crumb mixture over the top. Cover with foil and freeze until firm.

The fudge squares may be wrapped and frozen for up to several months.

* To serve, cut into 2½ x 2¼-inch squares.

SERVES 20